THE RING OF FIRE

Polynesian Seafaring

THE RING OF FIRE

Volume II

POLYNESIAN SEAFARING

*A Disquisition on Prehistoric Celestial Navigation
and the Nature of Seagoing Double Canoes
with Illustrations Reproducing
Original Field Sketches, Wash Drawings, or Prints
by Artists on the Early Voyages of Exploration
and Occasional Written Reports from On-the-Scene Observers*

EDWARD DODD

DODD, MEAD & COMPANY

NEW YORK   1972

ISBN 0-396-06522-8
Library of Congress Catalog Card Number: 70-38892
Printed in the United States of America

To all of the grandchildren in the hope that some of them may some day want to explore the wonders of Polynesia

He was there · Tangaroa was his name
All about him was emptiness
No where the land · No where the sky
No where the sea · No where man
Tangaroa called out · No echo to answer

Then in this solitude he became the world
This knot of roots it is Tangaroa
The rocks are he again
Tangaroa · The song of the sea
Tangaroa · He named himself
Tangaroa · Transparence
Tangaroa · Eternity
Tangaroa · The Powerful
Creator of the universe which is but the shell of Tangaroa
Who bestows on it life in beautiful harmony

Contents

PROVISIONING

NORTH/SOUTH VOYAGING

Foreword

A good friend of mine who is an eminent authority on Polynesia wrote, after reading an early draft of the manuscript, "What you have done in your writing is a lot of healthy speculating founded on your first hand knowledge of the Polynesian seas and of the Polynesian character, and on second hand knowledge of the history and culture." This book pretends to be no more than that. It propounds a theory of navigation that will perhaps be new to many readers although its roots are firmly anchored in myths, traditions, and in past records. This fore-and-aft star path theory is now dear to my heart, but I must claim for it only that it could have been a practical method for the ancient Polynesians. I cannot claim that it was actually employed by them; the evidence is too vague.

A reader will want to know an author's qualifications for writing a book of this sort which takes up the gauntlet against many noted scholars and writers.

After a boyhood of considerable small-boat sailing off the New England coasts, I had the good fortune upon graduating from Yale in 1928 to be able to acquire, in equal partnership with four other classmates, a downeast fishing-type schooner, the *Chance*, in which we set out to sail "around the world." I was thus able to spend a whole year traversing 10,000 miles across the Pacific Ocean in a vessel from which one could always, like a Polynesian of old, reach over the side and touch the water. During that year I made a study of celestial navigation and became so entranced with it that I was frequently accused of unnecessarily pinpointing our vessel like a battleship. Mine was the old Marcg Saint Hilaire method, woefully out of date these days but it served us well. On one occasion I even succeeded in crossing three stars on a point, a feat which is the seamen's equivalent of a hole in one on the golf course.

This first Polynesian adventure evidently planted a lasting seed for when I was able to semiretire from book publishing some dozen years ago, my wife and I made a hobby, or perhaps it might better be called a passion, of Polynesian culture. We engaged first off on a book on Polynesian art, the research for which took us to most of the ethnological museums of the world, most of them in Europe, many in the U.S.A. especially Hawaii, and in New Zealand. Our travels led us frequently to Polynesia where we have lived off and on with native families in Tonga and in Raiatea. But we have also roamed considerably in Hawaii, New Zealand, and the Marquesas as well as in our "home" islands, the Societies, visited Samoa, the Tuamotas, Rarotonga, and Fiji briefly but not infrequently and have even been as far afield as Easter and Madagascar. On the assumption that artistic and seagoing matters rarely meet between the covers of a book, I have borrowed occasionally from that book for this one, notably on the subject of Polynesian origins.

A number of books on different aspects of Polynesia has been planned, art, seafaring, mythology, that rare flower of the Temehani, the *tiare apetahi*, and perhaps some others. The title of the group is THE RING OF FIRE, the commonly known descriptive term for the volcanic and earthquake-girdled Pacific. This is Volume II.

The "second hand knowledge" has of course come from books, journals, manuscripts, and from talk. I have had the good luck to meet and in some cases to travel with a number of the outstanding anthropologists and archaeologists specializing in Oceania and I have been a dedicated reader and collector of books on Polynesia for many years. From the rare editions have come many of the pictures in this book but the more interesting ones are reproductions of original field sketches from museum and library collections. My principal library sources are listed in the *Bibliography* and any name unfamiliar to the reader will be identified there. I have deliberately avoided the scholarly practice of footnoting all sources specifically because I am not a professional scientist and want to make no seeming pretentions to academic rectitude. Where native terms are desirable or unavoidable I have used a sort of Polynesian *esperanto* without specifications of interchangeable t's and k's, r's and l's, or the confusing glottal stop. There is, perhaps, a bias toward Tahitian because that is the dialect most familiar to me and it seems closest to the old root language.

All that this book hopes to do is to cast a different ray of light on one sector of the murky mystery that has always surrounded the marvelous accomplishment of the Polynesian in finding his way to all of the widely scattered islands in the Great South Sea and to present a visual conception of the vessels which carried him there that is more complete and first-hand than other treatments of the subject.

Fetuna, Raiatea, December 1970

THE ARGUMENT

Drift and Accidental Voyaging

Of all the puzzles that challenge those who take an interest in the early cultures of man there are few as beguiling as the presence of the Polynesian in his Pacific islands. There he was when the European first discovered him nearly five hundred years ago and, now our latest radio-active carbon dates tell us, there he had been for some two thousand years previously.

Where did he come from and how did he get there?

Where he came from has been satisfactorily settled by the scientists; the physical and cultural anthropologists, the botanists, linguists, geneticists, and most lately the archaeologists. Their evidence is overwhelming; the ancestors of the Polynesian or proto-Polynesian originated in southeast Asia and migrated mostly by way of Indonesia and Melanesia to the ocean islands.

How he managed to get there has not yet been as conclusively resolved. This is not a primary concern of the genuine scientist. He knows who they are, where they came from. The logistics he leaves to the expert in such matters and to experienced students and authorities. They, not being able to apply true scientific disciplines to their conclusions, are not quite so sure. There are still enough unknowns lying about so that every so often an ingenious newcomer seems able to peddle an unconventional hypothesis that takes the public's fancy and even puts the scientist on the defensive.

The most recent of these are Thor Heyerdahl with his settlement from South America theory and Andrew Sharp with his accidental-voyage theory. Perhaps because of their simplicity such theories seem to have an instant appeal that sweeps aside the carefully accumulated evidence of the truth of the matter to gain a sudden popular following and turn a new spotlight on the islands of the ocean that have been quietly indifferent in the interim.

Heyerdahl's theory of South American origins was based largely on the assumption of what might be called *migration by drift*; the premise that travel could only be accomplished by following the prevailing winds and currents. He purported to "prove" this by drifting himself amidst much well-planned publicity from Peru to the Tuamotus on his raft *Kon-Tiki*. Later he supplemented this thesis with what he believed to be derivatives in stone-building techniques on Easter Island. His theory was patiently suffered and quietly discredited by the scientists on ethnological, not transportational, grounds but it still lingers in the mind of many a Hollywood fancier.

Andrew Sharp's theory is based on what might be called *migration by chance*; the premise that settlement was accomplished only by accidental blow-away voyages. Sharp is more scientific than Heyerdahl, and his massive, though post-European, statistics ingeniously presented have elicited wide respect among present-day navigators. Moreover his accidents have led him in the right directions from the right place, as Heyerdahl's did not. He is therefore tolerable to scientists who are not so much concerned with the "how" as they are with the "why" and "where." Nevertheless Sharp's theory has been convincingly shaken, though perhaps not entirely refuted, by Jack Golson's recent symposium on Polynesian navigation, a spirited debate in book form by six noted Pacific scholars and experts. But even so it, too, still lingers in the conservative scientific mind.

Both of these theories have been modified under pressure. Heyerdahl now grants Polynesian intrusions on Easter Island from the west, though he still apparently believes the first settlers came from America. Sharp has conceded that some islands may have been settled by canoes that were forcibly expelled by man rather than wholly by the whim of weather.

Neither of these theories gives much of any credit to the Polynesian for what some of us would like to call his "accomplishment" in populating the vast Pacific a thousand years or so before our European sailormen braved their own deep and dark blue waters.

This may be partly a matter of jealousy, for the European likes to nourish the illusion that he was the first to conquer the deeps. Indeed the south European is still reluctant to recognize the feats of his brother Viking, dismissing him as half legendary and any way impermanent compared to his more legitimate hero Columbus. Small wonder that he hesitates to credit a primitive Asian with an antecedence of two millennia or more and with the deliberate permanent settlement of islands more distant than any in his Atlantic. No, such a feat must be attributed to a sunken continent or to drift voyages on rafts before the prevailing winds or to accidental blow-aways of which only a pitifully small percentage can have survived.

The article on "Navigation" in the *Encyclopedia Brittanica* says that the earliest navigators are the Phoenicians around 600 B.C. and after them the Vikings 1200 years later. No mention is made of non-European voyagers of any sort. However in another article, one on "Polynesia," the inhabitants are granted to have achieved their islands in double canoes and radio-carbon dates are listed for the Marquesas in 124 B.C. and for Easter Island A.D. 536. Comparative distances are interesting: those "earliest" navigators, the Phoenicians, sailed short hitches in the island-studded Mediterranean inland sea; the Vikings island-hopped from the Shetland and Faroes to Iceland and Greenland over never much more than 300 miles of open water, although they did later on make splendid direct voyages of 1500 miles across the North Atlantic. The Marquesas are some 2000 miles from Samoa and Easter is well over a 1000 miles beyond the Marquesas.

The simple fact is that this extensive and largely homogeneous settlement was a long process, carefully premeditated in many of its stages and slowly but skillfully accomplished over successive periods of many hundred years. Ships had to be designed, built, tested, and redesigned. Means of navigating them had to be developed. Competent seamanship had to be learned. Methods of provisioning had to be perfected. Ways of carrying plants and animals for future colonies had to be devised. It must have been a very gradual process, experimental at first to relatively nearby islands. Consolidation of early gains and mastering of early skills must have been necessary before the longer distances were surmounted or the longitudinal voyages attempted.

Gradually as new islands and new groups of islands came to be discovered, there must have been born a faith that there were always new lands to be found. The risks were many but the rewards were great, and as successes accumulated over the centuries, new crews set forth with new hopes until every single spot of land on that ample ocean surface had felt the foot of Polynesian man.

By the time the European entered the Pacific, the last golden age of discovery was over and probably had been for several hundred years. There were no more islands; settlement had reached high tide and the old ways and old vessels were beginning to come to a dead end. Some scholars have felt that a process of degeneration had set in. Although this theory seems doubtful, even if it were true, there were probably vestiges enough for an anthropologist to have made accurate reconstructions of crafts and skills. But even after Cook the science of anthropology was still a hundred years in the making and by the time it matured enough to reach the Pacific, the relics had almost disappeared. So much so that their existence could be disbelieved altogether by the skeptics and had to be resurrected little by little from such ephemeral data as legends and linguistics, ancient adzes and fishhooks and works of art; remnants of old-time customs, ancestral genealogies, bone formations, burials and, most recently, radioactive carbon datings of archaic rubbish heaps.

All of these have been collected and studied by many scientists working in many distinct disciplines. Even today, nearly five hundred years after Magellan, new evidence is still coming to light. Most of these scientists sense an overall pattern and each one writes convincingly of his own stone in the masonry, but no one can seem to plug every gap in the dam that holds the waters of truth. Always there appears to be a weakness somewhere that can be exploited by a Heyerdahl or a Sharp to the satisfaction of at least a portion of the nonscientific public.

The weakness which seems to have been most expertly exploited is the crucial factor of seafaring. Here to a degree that occurs in no other aspect of the whole structure, the experts disagree. Most professional navigators declare that great ocean-going settlement voyages were impossible. It is the amateur sailors and the theoretical scholars who have endeavored to sustain the argument in this quarter.

This would seem to be uncertain ground; to claim that a broad theory can stand when the qualified experts in one important sector are preponderantly convinced that the theory cannot stand. This on the face of it might seem enough to overthrow any scientific proposition. That it does not do so is owing to the fact that we are trying to apply specialized knowledge in an attempt to be scientific when in this particular case scientific method is not applicable.

The real science of navigation on the waters of the earth, our own present-day system, is a relatively new technique that was conceived about five hundred years ago when the Renaissance or age of science was dawning in Europe. There had been astronomy reaching far back even into prehistory. Maps had been drawn. The concept of bearings of heavenly bodies projected onto flat surfaces of paper was an old astronomical concept, as old perhaps as the art or "science" of writing. But we must realize that it had not even been conceived of by many peoples of the earth. It was a symbol concept, one that had actual existence only in our heads, a "language" that could be useful only when translated into graphic form. From there it progressed with the discovery of the compass and later the chronometer to a highly refined and dependable method for finding one's exact place on a map of the world or a portion of it. Later it has been perfected with such elaborations as radar and loran and even satellites and has become so highly specialized technically that in practice it no longer has very much to do with the stars or the sun. It is now difficult for an expert in this field to conceive of navigation in any terms other than those of his own instruments and graphs. Indeed so automated have the commercial airlines become that navigators are now obsolete. With airlines replacing passenger and freight vessels only the lone amateur on his little sailing ship will soon be left to use the heavenly bodies and even he is now equipped with a new sextant attachment that enables him to take star sights in the day time.

But the important thing for us to remember is that the Polynesian did not write. He never measured angles. The entire concept of inventing signs and symbols, even of drawing a picture, was foreign to him. Petroglyphs were pictures and symbols but never developed into writing or phonetic writing except on Easter Island in post-European times under the stimulus of observing the European practice. Essentially the process of writing is an extension of the sense of sight. The devising of written symbols is a special and peculiar development of this sense which gives a whole new dimension to our culture and seems of such second nature to us that it might almost be classified as a separate sense in itself. It has been so useful to us that it is hard for us to conceive of the nonexistence of writing or graphic techniques. And we have become so dependent upon them that we have allowed our other senses to be neglected. The sense of graphic sight has dominated our brain. Only hearing has been able to hold its own. As a result one of the most important functions of the brain, memory, has been surrendered almost entirely to writing. All of our history, our law, our literature, our music, even our poetry, must be put on paper or microfilm, or even into the computer.

But this was not always so. Indeed in the ancient course of man's cultural evolution it is a very recent phenomenon. We should realize that penalties are imposed; that when writing records ancient legends and folklore, inventiveness stops. We must remember that man came a long, long way on his path without graphic symbols.

The Polynesian, one might say, came even further. He kept his stars and his islands fixed in his head as we keep them in tables and on charts. And for the purposes of his navigation perhaps this was an even more reliable method. Memory in whatever form is a highly civilized attribute. It bespeaks a man's appreciation of his learning and of his key to the future. It is one of the chief factors that distinguishes man from beast.

All of the so-called primitive people are noted for their memories, but it is probable that no culture has been known to develop this faculty to a greater extent than the Polynesian did. An old-time tale is told of a chief in Raiatea who had a restless and ambitious second son. Because his older brother was to inherit the land, the younger brother set forth in a fine double canoe well provisioned with fruits, animals, women, and male helpers. Four generations later a descendant of his returned to the valley in Raiatea. There he learned that the original older brother's family had died out, so he claimed the ancient homeland. They asked for proof of his rights and he recited without flaw the whole genealogy of the family, going back to the originating gods. He was accepted immediately and granted the chieftainship of the land.

14

*   *   *

Commenting (among other things) on their extraordinary memories, Captains S. P. Henry and J. R. Kent wrote in 1828: "The Tahytans are very cleanly in their persons, bathing three times a day in murmuring rivulets of fresh water, with which the island abounds, or else in the sea, which has a very gentle swell round the coast. Though thus passing an indolent voluptuous life, they are not gross, but imaginative, disposed to converse and reflect. The form of their religion is changed, but they are still Tahytans. Pohmaree left off drinking Kava, but he afterwards took to European liquors; and it was his delight to sit for long evenings together, along with his chiefs, over a bowl of grog, talking about Buonaparte, Captain Cook, King George, and foreign events . . . They know the Bible and Testament off by heart, from beginning to end, and they repeat the most dark and mysterious passages, till their eyes lose the film they had, and they can see, another world opening to them, beyond the gloom of this, as it were, by those awful corruscations which came down from above."

*   *   *

Writing is believed to have been developed first in the fertile crescent of Mesopotamia, later and independently in Egypt, China, etc. The reasons given for its inception are basically legal ones: the need of people, crowding together, to define the boundaries of their lands; another was the need for treaties defining the settlements of wars; still another and perhaps the most common was the need of money records and agreements in trade. None of these reasons was urgent to the Polynesian. He wanted no cities, not even towns; he lived in family groups scattered at natural intervals around the shores and up into the valleys of his islands. Boundaries were clearly defined by natural precipitous ridges. The conquered in warfare usually set forth to live elsewhere or mingled with the conqueror. There was no trade and thus no money, only a very vague though tremendously important custom of exchange of hospitalities and gifts whose proper balance was far better reckoned in the mind and heart than in figures on paper or *tapa*. In short, the Polynesian's way of keeping his records in his head rendered marks, signs, and numbers unnecessary. He communicated almost always in a face-to-face situation. He felt little need for writing two or three thousand years ago and it is quite apparent to anyone who knows him that he still feels little need for it today. His genealogies were the lawbooks of his land and his memory was the *Ephemeris, Nautical Almanac*, and other reference books of his art of navigation. Such a memory cannot be conceived of by our modern experts who are so dependent upon their graphics and therefore they cannot accept the Polynesian navigation.

Thus it becomes evident that our scientific ways are not applicable to nonliterate or nongraphic men and our experts must be disqualified from passing judgment in their own terms. These expert navigators are "scientists," in a science that does not touch the Polynesian. His navigation was a compendium of observation and memory, an art and skill that can no more be appraised by the captain of a freighter or a battleship than a chemist can assess the paintings of Gauguin.

What needs to be looked at afresh and explained in detail are the working techniques of this art of navigation, and that is no easy task. It must be done from pieces and clues taken from various monographs published in learned journals, from hints and records in the writings of early explorers, and from insights into the

15

Polynesian character. There will be attempted here a summary and simplification that, drawing on many sources, will hope to present a convincing whole.

The cases for drift and accidental voyaging presuppose, indeed they might be said to be founded on, the assumption that the early Polynesians were rather stupid, doltish types incapable of moving on the ocean except by drift and incapable of realizing that if they ventured out of sight of land, they would be likely to be blown away to kingdom come. Population by accidental voyages in as vast an area as the Pacific, with islands as small and scattered as they are, demands a staggering percentage of losses. There is probably no reliable way to estimate them but surely the chances of survival must have been at least one in a hundred, perhaps one in a thousand. That any well-equipped maritime people would tolerate such losses is incredible; the very fact that they were so well equipped negates the whole theory: one does not patiently construct beautifully conceived, deep-sea-going vessels in order to be blown away; any fool would simply have stayed ashore or cruised close by. If such losses occurred, they would have been expected and the Pacific would not have been populated . . . But it was. And huge ocean-going canoes were built. Abel Tasman saw them in 1642 when he discovered Tonga. And so did Cook in 1769. They were measured and drawn. They will be seen in this book. Why would anyone build such large canoes and go so far out if only one in a hundred survived?

No, let us suppose rather that the Polynesian was not the imbecile the skeptics see him, but a normal man of his time who could contest with his natural surroundings as well as another, perhaps better when he came to the sea. Let us inquire into the possible motivations that may have led him out over the blue water.

In my book on Polynesian art, on the assumption that anyone reading a new book on Polynesia should be entitled to a new theory on Polynesian origins, I developed a rather presumptuously wide-ranging theory derived from the many speculations I had read. There is actually nothing much new about it; it is, rather, a new composite of many old theories. Since those who read about the sea and those who read about art rarely meet each other between book covers and since in the ensuing years I have not been able to improve on that theory, nor has anyone come forth to disprove or even disapprove, I am going to summarize it here with minor revisions to suit a seafaring rather than an artistic atmosphere.

The salient characteristic that distinguishes the Polynesian from other human races, the main trait that picks him from his fellow men, is his seafaring. The other civilizations of the Great Ocean all came to their homelands on foot. When the australoids migrated into Australia perhaps some twenty millennia past, there were probably long low-water periods when the Indonesian islands and New Guinea were only higher points on a land mass that, except for Wallace's famous divide, stretched from Malaya to Tasmania. The same and also previous low-water periods would have laid bare a highway across Bering Strait in the north. It is a long walk from Mongolia over an interglacial bridge between Siberia and Alaska, down the cordillera of the Rockies, along the Isthmus and by way of the Andes to Cape Horn. But that is the way these men arrived. No short cuts; slow, steady plodding over thousands and thousands of years eventually overcame the thousands and thousands of miles. They bore their own burdens; there were no wagons to ride, probably no tame animals to help. Not that it was all, or even most of it, hardship. They were probably having a good time for the most part, plenty of game to hunt, new places to discover with untouched fruits, nuts, and roots, no need to worry about enemies or connections with a base back home. They were self-sufficient and free to improvise as they pleased. For centuries on end they had little need to plan ahead. That sort of movement, that sort of coping with daily ups and downs, that sort of adjusting to the dangers and opportunities of an immediate environment will show up in a man's character.

So will seafaring, a very different sort of locomotion. Firstly it postulates a more imaginative spirit with a greater capacity to plan ahead. It takes forethought to conceive of ocean-going canoes and it takes generations of skills to evolve and execute them. Moreover, it takes age-old knowledge of plants and their preservation to outfit and provision those canoes for weeks or more to come. Here is a cool, rational counterbalance to an impetuous impulse to go exploring the unknown, very different from wandering over the hill in sight of the campfire. Such projects involve important communal decision and cooperation. A departure is a crucial, emotional event; implying return and subsequent voyages, changes in families, new lands, new ways of life. Impassive resolution, yet sensitivity to danger, variety, and humor to pass the time gaily; ingenuity and grace to test or show skill; dignity, aloofness yet humility, summing up an independence of mind and spirit which is, however, ready to cooperate with one's fellow man and submit to social control. All these are ingredients of the seafaring personality.

Polynesian Origins

No one can venture into the subject of the Polynesians without running into countless speculations about their racial and geographical origins. This is not true of any of the ocean-rim people. Their pedigrees, with a few odd exceptions like the Ainu, are accountable enough, but the Polynesians have fascinated many a sailor, scholar, and scientist from Captain Cook, Banks, Bougainville, Vancouver, Rogeveen, and Dumont D'Urville to Peter Buck, Kenneth Emory, Thor Heyerdahl, Andrew Sharp, Roger Duff, and Gordon Lewthwaite. The Lost Tribes of Israel, the Dravidians and Munda of pre-Aryan India, the Ainu of Japan, the Incas of Peru, even the imaginary peoples of fabulous Gondwanaland have enjoyed their well-argued hours upon the speculative stage. The mystery will probably never be completely resolved, but modern scientists have lately been pulling aside more and more of the veils. It was customary not long ago to bewail the rapid dying out of a culture on the grounds that once it was gone we could never again learn as much about it. But the wisdom of Tylor, nineteenth-century father of the science of anthropology, is becoming ever more evident as old bones and bits of carbon are being dug up, namely that our knowledge of ancient peoples is growing more and more complete and intimate as the years go by. It is an exciting idea that we can look to the future for familiarity with the past.

One thing we can now be sure of: it is not so simple as it once seemed. A theory that accounts for complexities is therefore tempting to explore. Here is one.

Way back ten or twenty thousand years ago, one ancestral, proto-Polynesian nucleus in southeast Asia may well have been the rather timid river-mouth people. They left the right shaped adzes, which H. D. Skinner, the dean of contemporary Polynesian archaeology, has called the most revealing cultural fossil of ancient man. The adze is our most reliable clue; it is also the most inescapable one: you cannot postulate a man's origin or long residence in a land where you cannot find his adzes. The Polynesian's adze is as unique to him as our written language is to us and except in his present homeland, it is found nowhere else in the world but southeast Asia, including some of its offshore appendages such as the Philippines and Formosa, or in Indonesia.

These were the people who lived at the mouths and along the banks of the great rivers we now call the Irrawaddy, the Salween, the Chaupaya, the Mekong, and probably also the more northern Songkoi, perhaps also as far north and east as the Yangtze. They were the great gardeners of the old world, perhaps the first domesticators of plants and animals who founded the "hearths" of earliest agriculture. Here plants were first cultivated, the earliest ones from sprouts: bananas and plantains, taros, yams, coconuts, pandans, bamboos, sugar cane, breadfruit. These are the most ancient cultigens of the world and the list reads like an inventory of a modern Polynesian homestead.

18

OLD WORLD PLANTING AND HOUSEHOLD ANIMALS

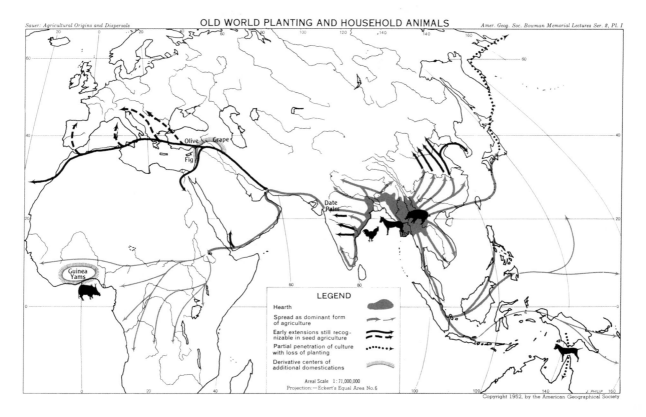

LEGEND

Hearth

Spread as dominant form
of agriculture

Early extensions still recognizable in seed agriculture

Partial penetration of culture
with loss of planting

Derivative centers of
additional domestications

Areal Scale 1:71,000,000
Projection:—Eckert's Equal Area No.6

Here the first animals were domesticated: the pig, the chicken, and the dog. From this area they spread throughout the world; west where they met and mingled with the later domesticates of India and Mesopotamia, the ass, horse, camel, cattle; northeast into China, but only the dog went over the bridge into the Americas. Southeast in Polynesian canoes they traveled over the whole Pacific. Some of them even ventured directly across the ocean to be adopted into the new world hearth; coconuts and plantains came through the tropics from the tropical west to join the indigenous corns and squashes, turkeys and llamas. Only a few went back: cucumbers and gourds, and most important to the Polynesians, the ubiquitous sweet potato.

The characteristics that seem to spring from these river-mouth people are patience and a foresight that beckoned them to cut shoots and plant for the year ahead; then to watch these reproductions year after year, decade after decade, century after century; to select the mutations that suited them best, to isolate and breed them for all the variety of qualities that we find available to us today.

The popular nineteenth-century assumption that all this experimentation was motivated by necessity, that these people were living on the brink of subsistence, is smiled at by modern scientists. With all our laboratories, techniques, time, and money we have not begun to be as prolifically inventive as these old world people. The scores of varieties of banana that we may enjoy today (if we are epicurean in the bananic realm) were developed for sheer pleasure, out of sheer virtuosity. The natural potential seems always to be present. When our American ancestors cleared our forests for their families, at least one-hundred eighty varieties of hawthorn

19

burst from only a few formerly frustrated varieties. But our hawthorn exploded inadvertently; their bananas were guided by a wise and loving, selective hand, so rigidly guided that they lost their ability to produce fertile seed.

What were these people like? They were patient. They were well regulated socially or domestically. They were protected and thus they tended to their own business and stuck to their own sections of land. Except for sporadic periods of internecine warfare, probably caused by overpopulation pressures, they were at peace and for the most part peaceful. All this adds up to constancy.

They had foresight and they were experimental so they must have had an element of adventure in them. It seems now almost certain that the original motive for taming the dog, the chicken, and even the pig was one of pleasure, challenge, companionship. Only the very young animals could be taken from the wild, and they had to be suckled by the women along with their own children. It was not until much later, when domestication was not only complete but perhaps even tiresome, that these pets were raised for food. This would indicate an innate sense of playfulness and companionability, a kinship with fellow living creatures.

They were specialized artisans. Their skills and their way of life must have meant much to them. If attacked they would probably not want to share them with others; it was a difficult if not impossible kind of life to share with an enemy even if they were his slaves. Logically they would be easily defeated. With their foresight and patience, they would most likely move away if a strong intruder approached. And so these river-delta, agriculturalist fishermen may have been forced south by fiercer folk from the west and north, into the island-studded Java Sea.

We know that about 3600 years ago the great Aryan overland invasions were taking place, that the conquerors came down from the mountainous plateaus of Iran above Mesopotamia to subdue India and to found its present dominant caucasoid strains. Since the descending Aryans were strictly landsmen, it seems unlikely that they could have come also as a flanking group by sea. But as they swarmed from the plateaus of Iran in great hordes, it is not unlikely that they would drive the older, fellow-caucasoid, river-mouth people of the Tigris and Euphrates, who were also coastal sailors of the Indian Ocean, to the eastward, to Ceylon, Malaya, and Indonesia.

There, let us speculate, they might have mingled with the mongoloid agriculturalists that had been forced down from the great peninsula of southeast Asia, both groups fugitives from continental throngs.

It is possible, of course, that the caucasoid-mongoloid mixture took place with the Aryan invaders before or during the time that the river-delta people were being displaced. The Aryans could have accounted for the caucasoid elements in a resulting melange. But in this case it would be upland landsmen mixing with sea-coast landsmen and it is a firm premise of this book that the most important characteristic of the resulting Polynesian is his oceanic seafaring. Where did he pick up this all-important trait?

It is conceivable that he developed it himself in the Indonesian islands. This sprawling complex of water-spaced lands must have made a great training ground for sailors. Life would have been relatively secure from the continent dwellers for a while at least, several centuries perhaps of isolation before new land-based stresses would develop.

On the other hand a strain of caucasoid fugitives from the southern seashores of

The two most common types of canoes in Polynesia were the single-hulled outrigger and the double hull, both types with or without sails. These are from Tonga by James Webber, c, 1777.

Mesopotamia may have been seafarers long since. The open salt-water, ocean sailing off the river-delta mouths of the two great Mesopotamian rivers presented a challenge very different from the inland seas of southeast Asia or Indonesia. At first they were probably coastal sailing folk, but soon the kindly beam winds of the Indian Ocean monsoons would beckon them onto the blue waters. The ancient Phoenicians had perhaps been their mentors, for it is known that later on the Arabs and Greeks hired Phoenicians to build their boats and sail them. And it is also known that Phoenicians constructed vessels bottom upward from hewn-out logs and built-up plank sides. What is not known and is most mysterious is the conception of the double canoe or what we now inappropriately call the catamaran.* What a marvelous invention it was! Born of necessity? More likely for the sport of it. Captain Cook relates with wonder how the Tongan chiefs literally sailed rings around his ship even when she was doing her best in a fair breeze. But soon afterward the double hull was virtually forgotten and allowed to rot for hundreds of years. It is only now beginning to be appreciated again for its speed, maneuverability, and steadiness at sea.

*The word "catamaran" originated in Malaya and meant literally "tied logs," a kind of float or raft used to surmount the offshore surf. The subsequent use of the term to define a twin-hulled vessel seems no more appropriate than its further alternative dictionary meanings, "a vixen, a scold or a quarrelsome woman."

The double-hulled and outrigger types must have originated in Indonesia; whether indigenously or from a "break-through" adaptation of Phoenician-type water craft we shall probably never know. But considering the admixture of racial strains and of maritime skills, the theory of a commingling or diffusion of talents rather than totally independent development seems persuasive.

The third type of Pacific canoe was the double outrigger, but this occurred only in Indonesia. There is no record of one of these ever having been seen in Polynesia. Drawing by Webber.

A fourth type, ordinary to us, is, of course, the broader single hull without outrigger. This did occur in Polynesia, but only in Maori New Zealand where tree trunks were large enough. Almost always they were war canoes.

Coastwise
Versus Bluewater Sailing

H ere is perhaps as good a place as any to set out upon a digression on the very important distinction between the two kinds of people in the world who make boats and sail them. Three distinctions might be drawn if inland-water people were included, but artful though the fresh-water canoeists were, they will be set aside from this discussion.

The two species of *homo aquiens* are: (1) the coastwise sailor, (2) the ocean-going or blue-water sailor. Most landsmen think this division is a quibble, but it is not. The basic, psychological natures of the two types are radically different, as different as the mountain climber from the spelunker, or the airplane pilot from the driver of a tank, or the poet from the painter. This is not to say that one is inferior to the other, but to emphasize that there are fundamental and clearly discernible differences.

This may be a slippery thesis to prove, but it is a pleasurable one for speculation, and a failure to recognize this coastwise versus blue-water distinction has resulted in many misconceptions about Polynesian migrations. It lies at the base of Andrew Sharp's accidental-voyage fallacy. It is one of the strongest supports for the thesis that Jack Golson has argued so well and that so many eminent, though nonnautical, anthropologists like Peter Buck, Kenneth Emory, and Roger Duff have taken on faith. It is, however, a point of pertinence that has not been examined carefully nor clearly defined. The definition is not easy. The argument depends on intangible, almost spiritual factors, the kind that are immediately suspect to the skeptics. That there exists a valid and important distinction is obvious only to the so-called blue-water sailor. When he tries to point that out, he is subject to suspicion of taking a position holier than thou.

The history books of the Western world will tell you that long-range voyaging began in the eastern Mediterranean, first perhaps the boatmen of the Nile in their feluccas and the fabulous voyages down the Red Sea and along the Indian Ocean shores to Ethiopia and even to Mozambique to fetch back gold and slaves from black Africa. Next the Phoenicians are lauded for their daring voyages the length of the Mediterranean. The Carthaginians fetched back lead from Ireland, and so on . . . All of these venturers are supposed to have ardously accumulated, over a thousand years or more, the know-how that finally enabled Vasco da Gama and Columbus to break loose from the land and sail the ocean deeps. The Norsemen are presumed to have built up their own techniques independently in the cold Northland.

Thus all of our ancient maritime roots are coastwise. The Phoenician was considered the most daring because he could sail out of sight of land for several days on end. But never forget that he knew exactly where he was going. All the Mediterranean shores had been carefully explored by cautious coasters beforehand. He was not sailing into the unknown; he was only taking a short cut, a wise thing to do, but one that did not require any real departure from his regular coasting techniques, only an extension of them that amounted to little more than additional food.

The coastwise sailor keeps the land always in view or always close enough so that, weather allowing, he can bring it into view whenever he chooses. This is a dangerous business. There are rocks and reefs and shoals offshore that can sink or trap a boat with almost no warning. Unpredictable, changeable, variable currents swirl about the fringes of land: water currents are most perilous, but air currents are treacheous too. Then, if a ship is wrecked or forced to land, hostile inhabitants were the frequent expectation.

All of these things make the coastwise sailor a jumpy fellow, one who is suspicious and constantly on the lookout for trouble, wary and cautious. Since his business is from port to port depending on many factors, he is also an improviser, taking on cargoes and getting rid of them subject to whims. Thus, except for cargoes, and they have little to do with seamanship, there is not much need to plan far ahead. When trouble brews, the coaster tends to head for harbor and to lay up until the sky clears. Thus there is not much need for self-reliance at sea. The coaster's navigation is all oriented to the land. He takes bearings constantly, measures his progress by the points of land that he passes, measures his distances by eye. Indeed he relies first and foremost on the sense of sight. He must and does at times develop a fine sense for hearing breakers and detecting rips and swirls. In fog an old down-Easter summons up a symphony of senses: hearing, touch, smell, and taste that serve him better than radar. All of these are highly specialized and closely tied to the land.

His rhythms are periods of acute, constant awareness when at sea, alternating with slothful security when at anchor. This makes him a hand-to-mouth man, catch-as-catch-can; an improviser, an externalist, a doer with little time for contemplation or philosophy. He would not have much use for farming or growing things ashore. He is, in short, an amphibian.

The blue-water sailor by contrast is a long-range fellow. Perhaps like the whale, he has chosen to adapt himself to a new natural environment. After careful, interminable preparation, his first aim is to get away from the shore and its attendant perils, to launch himself on the good, safe, ocean deep. All of your Andrew Sharps assume that the high seas are a region of danger, of fear of the unknown, of sudden storms and of ever-threatening oblivion. Quite the contrary. A blue-water man never feels safe and content until he is a couple of hundred miles offshore. In our Atlantic country this is where the continental shelf with its gray-green water ends, the line where the clear blue waters of the open ocean begin. These color gradations are much more abrupt for the Polynesian, but the principle is the same. He, too, needs a hundred miles or so to forget his worries about a lee-shore blow.

Once free, the ocean sailor settles down to a blessedly regular, daily round. The ship is cleansed of its contaminating land dirt; the hatches are battened down against the possibility of the stormiest seas; watches are set. The classic intervals of day and night are replaced by three eight-hour cycles that shuffle the twenty-four-hour interval evenly. Sleeping, eating, working, playing go in these cycles of their own pretty much regardless of light and darkness. The significance of this break with the landsman's tradition is not always appreciated, but it is complete. It bespeaks an independence, and it results in an entirely different rhythm of life. Instead of conforming to the basic elements of day and night, you make them conform to you. You split them up, rotate the splits with dog watches, and partake equally, in progression, of the light and the dark. You come to know and become enamored of the ever-changing starlit night. You become bored with the monotonous day.

Of course we do not know that the Polynesian set eight-hour watches and dogged them, but we can be pretty certain, from the way he uses time ashore today, that he did something of the sort. It is the only way that has ever worked at sea. It is the only way that can work. Whereas the coastal sailor engages in intense activity and observation during the daylight hours and must relax in port or run offshore and heave to for the night, the deep-sea sailor spreads his energy and activity evenly regardless of the comings and the goings of the sun.

The open ocean is not a region of terror for the blue-water sailor. Far from it; it is a region of security. He knows, of course, that there is danger in a great storm, but he knows that great storms are rare and that even if they strike, he has the wisdom and skill to give himself a good chance. He is no more fearful of sudden death from storms at sea than a landsman is of being smashed up in an automobile accident. They both happen, but we do not live in dread of either one. Nor do we hesitate to set forth and take our chances.

"But," goes the argument, "how about that primitive fellow in his frail canoe? He was in a much more precarious state than our modern liner or last century's clipper ship or even the vessels of Columbus and Vasco da Gama." Not so. There is an almost universal conviction amongst landsmen that the smaller the boat, the greater the danger. Everyone who has sailed the high seas in a small boat knows that this is untrue for a hundred reasons, but he knows also by now that the nonbeliever can never be convinced by logical argument or even by demonstrable proof. You must sail yourself for days and nights on end with only a foot or so of freeboard to know how safe it feels close to the bosom of the sea.

It is tempting to speculate where blue-water sailing was born, where elements of the proto-Polynesians might have learned their sea-going arts even before they arrived in Indonesia. An ideal region is the Indian Ocean, where the monsoons are not only as dependable as any winds on earth, but they reverse directions each season, so that one can sail out on a beam wind from the southwest in the summer months and back on a northeast beam wind in the winter. To take a short cut across the open sea required only the skill of building larger and stronger vessels and the art of reading the stars at sea in a manner akin to that of ancestors who had long been traversing the desert.

And so the Mesopotamian Aryan might have developed, even on the muddy Indian Ocean, blue-water sailing skills and a blue-water psychology, well before the highland Aryans came down from Iran to conquer their seaports and send them east and south to the Indonesian islands where they would meet the rivermouth men from Indonesia.

Both of these groups would have been races that tended to live apart, absorbed in their own intricate occupations. A mixture of these horticultural offshore fishing mongoloids with deep-sea caucasoids, and perhaps a peppering of local australoid, would then have become the so-called Malayo-Polynesian people in the Indonesian islands about four or five thousand years ago.

Later on another aggressive, fast-multiplying race of little men, this time more likely from the large lands of the Chinese north, could have borne down upon these island people. The islanders may have been diffident or even cowardly, possibly just peaceable. In any case, as before, rather than stand and die, or surrender and mix, they chose to take to their ocean-going canoes. Around about three thousand to four thousand years ago perhaps, while the Druids were ferrying huge stones from Wales to Britain, when the later Trojan wars were being fought on the shores of the Aegean Sea, when Moses was leading his chosen people out of Egypt to the Promised Land, these people began to disperse. All over the world these were times of stirrings among men.

A branch, probably much later, went southwest to Madagascar to found the Imerina and Betsileo tribes on the high central plateau, the choice soil of the land. From there their chieftains, the Hova, taught their musical language to all the successive migrations from Arabia, Africa, India, and Malaya, so that the nine million polyglot peoples of the Great Red Island all speak the same Malayo-Polynesian language. Naturally enough after a separation of perhaps fifteen hundred years from Indonesian origins it has changed considerably since the primary influx, or at least it differs noticeably from the Pacific dialects, but its roots and many of its more universal words are unmistakably the same today.

The main procession of Pacific migrants probably coasted southwards along the huge Melanesian island of New Guinea and its southeastern outliers to fetch their first oceanic homelands of Fiji, Samoa, and Tonga. Others, later on, may have arched further north through the Micronesian atolls. At least one element in the eventual Polynesian pudding probably came from further up the Chinese coast by way of Taiwan and Luzon. Skinner has found a continuing trail of adzes and clubs that mark that route. Many must have stopped along their ways to mix with indigenous australoids, leaving traces of softer dialects and lighter skins especially along the coastal areas, and picking up darker skins, fuller lips, and sometimes kinky hair. Some stayed behind long enough to leave their influences still in such south Indonesian islands as the Mentawai, especially Nias and Enggano. Later on some came back to impose their dominant, oceanically evolved Polynesian traits in such Micronesian islands as Nukuoro and Kapingamerangi. Others took over small, scattered, nonmalarial islands like Tikopia, within the Melanesian groups.

Nothing of the Polynesian physical traits remains recognizable in present-day Indonesia; only traces of their language which still persist and certain basic religious concepts such as the male staff wrapped in the female bundle as the symbol of the completed universe.

So, then, this seafarer who dared the mighty ocean deeps was born, perhaps, of gentleness and fear, more likely of a desire for independence and escape, with supposedly a generous admixture of the patient traits extending over generations that must have gone into the genesis of the green thumb.

But if fear of other men or a distaste for mingling too intimately with them propelled him forth, courage to conquer the elements fetched him to his new, far-distant ocean home where other men were left behind. It often seems that men who love nature and men who love the sea tend to stay apart from other peoples.

And there in the Pacific, let us suppose, this peaceful fellow settled down for a long while, probably many centuries. No other man had the skill to sail across his wide, blue moat. So it was there in the central islands of the ocean that his ancestral Asian traits with their caucasoid intrusions must have gradually evolved into what we now distinguish as the Polynesian race. In time his own population pressures built up. His old, never-abandoned navigational traditions tested his patience, strained his marvelous memory, to take him over the seas again in successive waves and pulsations of centuries' durations to the farthest fragment of land on the face of the Great Ocean.

There is too much speculation and induction in this very broad bifurcal theory to give it much appeal to the skeptic, but it does account for four important, self-evident, perhaps overriding facts:

1. The hard scientific trail of quadrangular and triangular adzes from eastern and southern Indochina.

2. The important existence of an ancient and honorable nonseeding, sprout-propagating horticultural heritage.

3. The presence of substantial caucasoid as well as mongoloid blood.

4. The much overlooked, but critical element of an extraordinary deep-sea tradition.

When he first came to these islands, these safe, smiling, virgin, volcanic and coralline lands, he brought with him two hereditary traits that seem to be clearly Polynesian: the complex trait of his seafaring nature predicated on adventure-someness, foresight, navigational art generated from memory and tradition; and the relatively simple trait of peaceableness, a rooting, growing instinct that craved security.

It seems probable that he also brought a third, more mysterious, emotional ingredient; his religion and mythology, because it appears to reach so far back into his past. Whether he brought it to his islands ready-made or whether he perfected it after he arrived there, it was surely of primary importance to the fundamental pattern of his nature. It provided him with an emotional spectrum that blended the natural with the supernatural, freeing him from the excessive fears that obsessed the landsmen of the continental shores. His faith made death not an end, but a transition to ancestor worship and thence to spirits and to gods. It assured him a calm, underlying philosophy for a balanced, social stability.

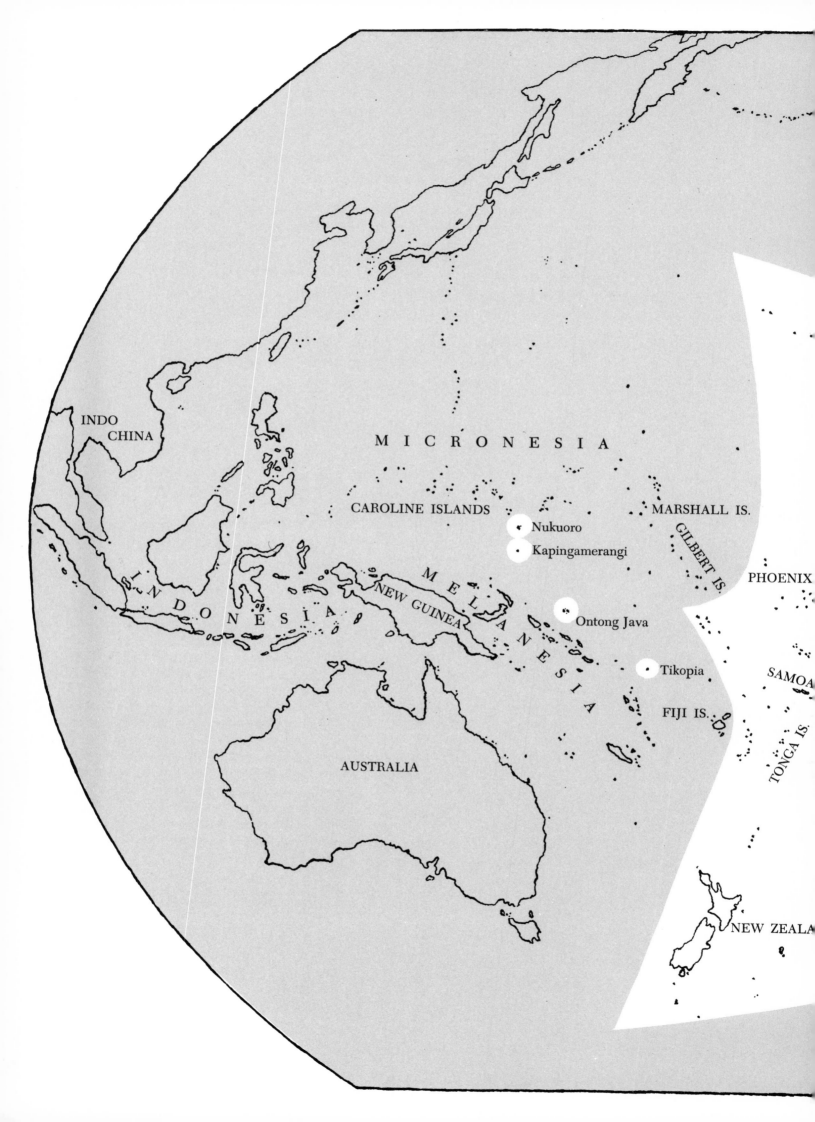

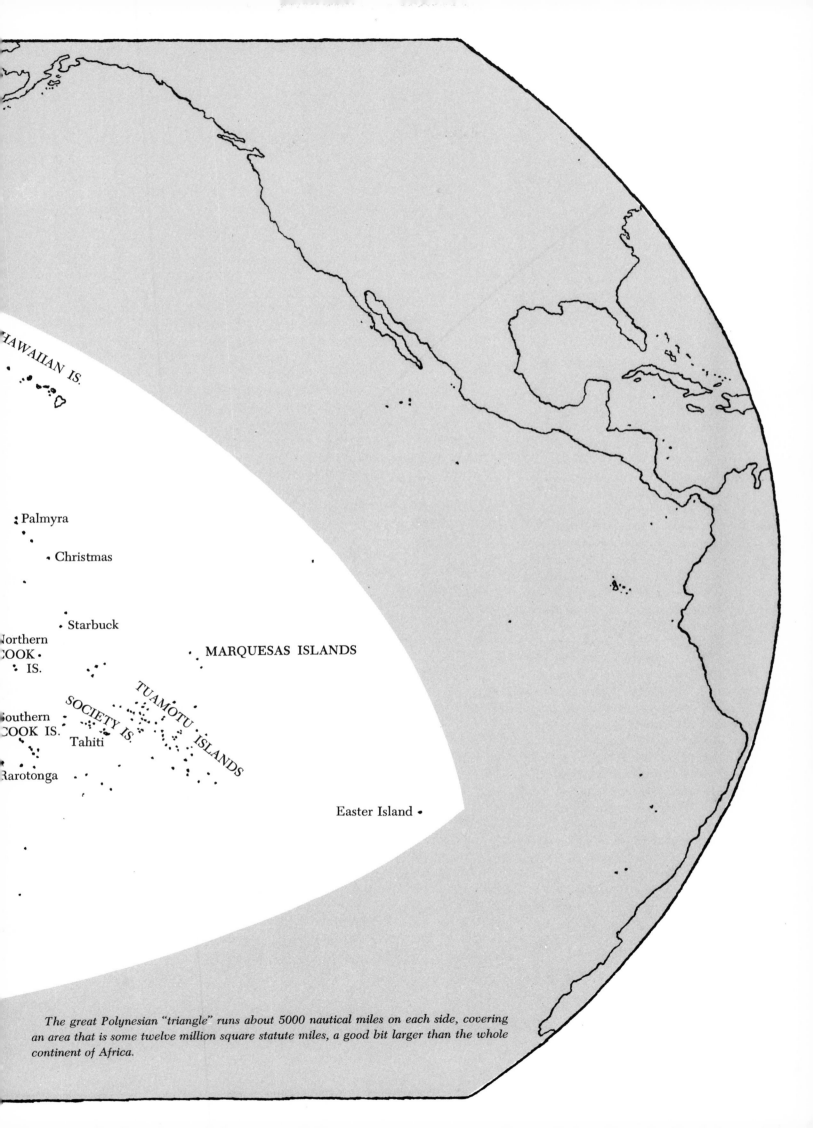

HAWAIIAN IS.

Palmyra

Christmas

Starbuck

Northern
COOK
IS.

MARQUESAS ISLANDS

TUAMOTU

SOCIETY IS.

ISLANDS

Southern
COOK IS.
Tahiti

Rarotonga

Easter Island

The great Polynesian "triangle" runs about 5000 nautical miles on each side, covering an area that is some twelve million square statute miles, a good bit larger than the whole continent of Africa.

Motivations

Now let us assume that about four thousand years ago (2000 B.C.), having been invaded from the north, the proto-Polynesian took to his boats. A splinter portion slanted southwest across the Indian Ocean to Madagascar. After an initial eastward movement, these seem to have turned back from Borneo or Celebes about 1000 A.D. But naturally the main body would go on eastward. To the west and north lay his populous enemies, to the south lay open water and cold weather, to the east he was beckoned by the island stepping stones of Melanesia and Micronesia. But the great Melanesian islands had long before been populated by australoids (Papuans) and, perhaps more important, the country proved to be malarial. The Micronesian islands were too small and too barren to invite any but emergency settlement and yet some of those who eventually gave rise to the Polynesian peoples probably took this route. Or perhaps some set out separately from the more northern coastal regions of southeast Asia and never went through Indonesia at all. The Philippines would have been training grounds almost as salubrious for incipient seafarers as Indonesia and an original common culture could be assumed to develop in similar ways. But most of them probably sailed eastward, skirting through Melanesia to the first great oceanic cluster, Fiji, Samoa, and Tonga. There they found rich virgin land, plenty of it, to support them for several hundred years.

Why did they go further? Not only further, but further and further until they became geographically the most widely dispersed race on the earth?

What were their motivations? (1) Love of adventure, (2) exploration, (3) conquest of land, (4) conquest of people, (5) colonization, (6) escape? These seem to have been their root reasons, but to understand them better we might add and eliminate some motives that were, or are, significant in ourselves, (7) proselytizing or religious conversion, a motive that never seems to have moved them, though it has sent us into the frenzies of Islam, the self-righteousness of Christianity and the seduction of Buddhism. And finally, (8) our most pervasive and compelling motivation; trade. We must virtually rule that out in our assessment of the Polynesian, but this is not an easy cultural excision to make. Trade is basically embedded in us. Perhaps its pernicious ways are not easily perceptible in the Vikings, but in all the other great seafaring groups of our cultures it is probably paramount. It sent the Arabs from the Golden Horn for tea and spices to Ceylon, the Carthaginians to Ireland for lead, the Portuguese to India for spices and precious stones, Columbus to America for gold, Captain Cook to the Pacific for land, and in his wake the Nantucketers for whales and the traders for sandalwood; soon after it sent the slavers to Africa for what they considered subhuman blacks. The Arctic and Antarctic adventurers were probably the least contaminated by Mammon, for

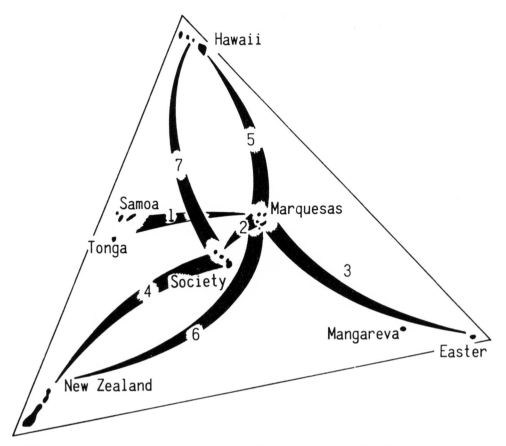

Diagram of primary settlement pattern of East Polynesia implied by recent archaeological findings. Kenneth Emory and Yosi Sinoto, 1965.

even the Vikings had plunder in mind. Is the chance of exploitation of new minerals and chemicals a part of our present yearning for the moon?

You cannot call accidental voyaging motivated unless you count forced exile which can be classed as escape. These motivations are listed above as if they were all different, as if some canoes were moved by one, some by another. Of course they were actually combined and interrelated, some being dominant in some circumstances, others in different ones. Whether or not the voyages were premeditated, however, all of them were dependent for their success upon two critical factors, *weather* and *navigation*. By the skeptics who cannot accept deliberate two-way voyaging, weather and navigation are fundamental uncertainties, so uncertain that they cannot believe that "primitive" men could overcome them. But these convictions derive from two hypotheses that may be somewhat insecure: namely, that movement must always follow the winds and currents, and secondly that if the Polynesian ventured forth into the unknown, he had no means of finding his way back. Actually neither of these factors may have been as uncertain as is generally assumed.

Winds and Weather

Weather is, of course, uncertain from day to day, but it is not, when you mind it well, uncertain from week to week, especially in the well-established lunar cycles of medium range, say three, four, five weeks. We all know our monthly weathers with fair certainty. "March comes in like a lion and goes out like a lamb." "Whan that Aprille with his shoures sote/ The droghte of Marche hath perced to the rote." "April showers bring May flowers." "What is so rare as a day in June?" And in a longer range we all know what kinds of summers, autumns, and winters we are likely to have in our respective earthly regions. We will have an extra-dry summer or an extra-warm winter, but the variation is not great, and once a season gets under way it is reasonably predictable. Writers on Polynesian navigation who listen to the old sea captains are receiving their data from freighters, trading ships, warships, passenger vessels; boats that have taken their captains where they wanted to go, when they wanted to go there. All are engine-driven and thus relatively immune to weather conditions. Naturally they encountered all kinds; naturally they remember the worst of it. They do not stop to realize that the Polynesian set forth only when the weather suited him. He had no schedules to meet, no cargoes to deliver within specified dates, no overhead to liquidate. So he sailed when the sailing was good. He stayed at home in stormy times. And as all the early observers testify, he was an uncanny weather prophet.

We are accustomed in our corner of the earth to reckon weather in terms of hot or cold, wet or dry. These were almost insignificant to the Polynesian; perhaps not to the crop grower, but we are concerned with the seafarer. Winds and storms were his prime concern. The well-know oceanographer, William Van Dorn, says, "... the mean climate in *mid-ocean* is remarkably uniform compared with that over continents."

Our ancestors knew their winds much better than we do. Nowadays the breezes make themselves conspicuous only in certain fairly well-defined areas and at certain regular seasons. Even our hurricanes have their habits: July stand by, August watch out; September remember, October all over. There is the mistral in southern France, the sirocco in Italy, the monsoons in southern Asia, and always over the equatorial oceans the faithful trades. These are all readily predictable; this is certain, not uncertain weather. If you can tolerate a bit of changeableness in two- or three-day spurts, you know moderately well how it will average out over any particular moon, and even better over any particular season. Beyond that, real uncertainty sets in; we cannot predict the year's weather and therein lies fear for the land-bound cultivator but not, luckily, for the deep-sea sailor. His concern is for the season and the month within the season, and for the day to day. There is scarcely any place on this earth where he cannot, with average luck, within an average season, sail from any reasonable departure point to any destination within an average month at an average speed of 70 or 80 miles a day; assuming, of course, that he has at least an average intelligence; that he is not a stunt performer setting out from New Zealand to Cape Horn just to be sensational.

An interesting speculation which, as far as I know, has received very little attention beside passing remarks is the state of the weather a couple of thousand years ago when the Polynesian was making most of his long voyages. They all agree that it was probably much warmer and more benign than it is today. Hornell, our foremost authority on the watercraft of Oceania, found the recurved bailer handle and a certain type of plank fastening, both of them otherwise unique to Indonesia and Polynesia, in an isolated fishing community in Scandinavia. To account for them he writes that it is possible that in a previous millenium the world weather was enough warmer so that Polynesians or proto-Polynesians could have sailed around the north coast of Siberia to Europe. We know that an extensive and prolonged worsening climate around 1000–800 B.C. gradually drove the Alpine lake dwellers from their platforms raised on piles dispersing them even as far north as Britain and destroying their way of life. It also had a notable and disastrous effect on European agriculture. Here is a specific, datable change of climate on a wide scale, almost certainly world wide, and it may have had significance for Polynesian migrations.

Virtually all writers when commenting on navigation or related maritime matters give the Polynesian "credit" for knowing the points of the compass and often take careful pains to note the names given to all the directions around the disk, observing that the Polynesians had specific, definite terms for at least the sixteen primary points and that these names indicated a surprisingly sophisticated knowledge. But of course here again the European is defining things after his own fashion. The Tahitian knew and named a great many directions, but it was only by coincidence that they had anything to do with our compass. Varela in 1774-1775 started the misunderstandings by noting carefully each native term as he boxed his compass. And there was indeed a name for every direction in which he pointed, or at least they obliged him with one. He failed, however, to realize that there were many more as well. Other explorers performed the same experiment and the results for the most part came out with enough consistency to convince subsequent observers that in this respect at least, the Polynesian was scientific in a European sense. Only one seems to have understood the real state of affairs, E. S. Craighill Handy. This is not surprising, because he is a perceptive cultural ethnologist and I suspect he does not care very much about the dictates of compasses. His "wind rose," if you can call it that, comes out with twenty-three "points" and in good Polynesian fashion they are irregularly distributed. About the only resemblance to a compass are the four inescapable cardinals, North, South, East and West, but from the names that adjoin them it seems evident that even these had variable ranges.

In comparing the best source of direction names; Varela, Davies, Henry, Gill, Handy, and Churchill; it is interesting to note that out of some fifty choices, only eleven are common to two or more of them and, of these, at least three have widely swinging meanings. *Toerau* varies from West by South to North. *Huatau* means strong Northwest to Davies and South by East to Handy. *Niuhiti* or *niufiti*

Niuhiti no Pare
Toerau farara
Apa toerau or toerau nia
Maoae farara toerau
Pahaapiti or Faarua
Papaa ite
Hau iti no Teriitua
Maoae tarava
Tooa o te ra or toerau rahi
or Toerau tia
Toerau tairoto
WEST
NORTH
EAST
SOUTH
Hitia o te ra
or Maoae tahiri
Maraamu moana
or Maraamu tahuareva
Fee tietie
Tarava iti or Temuri
Fee ti
Arue roa
Hauviri
Maraa'i
Maraamu maraa
Maraamu tairoto
Huatau
Maraamu faravao
Apa toa or Toa a Ahurei

Chart of wind names by E. S. C. Handy, 1932. E. G. R. Taylor says that it is clear that the wind rose came only after the magnetic compass circa 1390.

means Northeast to Davies and Northwest to Handy.

All of this tells us, I think, that the Tahitian knew well his winds and all their subtle variations, but that characteristically he knew them not as a system but as individuals, by their traits or habits as much as by their directions.

The Four Winds

O North Wind!
Evoked from the abyss
Driving the scudding clouds over the unsailed horizons.
A Wind,
Made known in the onrush of cloud banks
    fleeing before the fury of the blast,
Whose tempestuous breath
    swells the surging chaos of the sea.

O North Wind!
You come from the Primeval Source
    trembling in the first throes of creation,
While the divine seed of life, there—far below,
Impregnates the womb of the winds!

You come, red-washed in the streamers of the sunset,
Trailing cloud banners,
    torn in the consummation of your desire.
Evoke your rapture till the oceans seethe and toss!
    Oh, divine ecstacy!

II. East Wind

O East Wind!
Born of the abyss,
Conceived in the womb of the universe
    pregnant with the winds.
A Wind,
Holding steadily over wide wastes of remote oceans,
And revealed in the tempest
    of storm-heads and scurrying rain.

O East Wind!
You burst forth into the world of light,
While, far below,
The life generating waters
    explore the primeval source of the divine surge of life.

O East Wind!
O visible rapture of the Towering One
    mated with the Eternal Goddess!
You come from the age-old realm of the noble dead.

You have carried out your life bestowing labors
    upon the widespread, welcoming Earth,
While ever your winds strive together
    in the primordial cup of life,
Convulsed in the sacred union of the gods.
                Oh, assuagement of divine desire!

III. South Wind

O South Wind!
"Mighty-Wind-of-the-South" was the name
    of your bleak and frigid breath in times of old,
Holding steadily over diminishing ranges
    reaching to far horizons.

O South Wind!
Of you it was said, in ancient times:
"The south wind is the breath
    of him who leans upon the lightning!"

You are the wind honored in song
    by the young women of our clan, chanting:
"O Mighty-wind-of-the-south!
How bitterly cold is your breath!
How bleak is the wind
    fingering the crowded peaks
    and frosting the pathway winding along the shore!"
You are the wind arousing the wife
    to the warmth of love, as she sings:
"O my husband!
Now build a fire upon our hearth
    to warm us this night;
Come to my straining arms—wrapped in your patterned quilt
    stained with yellow turmeric designs,
And fragrant with blossoms of the creeping vine,
While we cling together, O my lover!
Embracing, flaming with ardor—
            Swooning in the sacred fire!"

IV. West Wind

O West Wind!
You dwell in the deep caverns of the realm of night;
Sharp is your chilly breath
Coming from ocean wastes, beyond the setting sun,
    where storm clouds gather.

O West Wind!
Ever you abide in the primeval chasm,
Roiling the tidal flow with white sands
    flung up from your ocean bed.

A Wind,
Dying down into the gentle, westerly breeze,
    wafted from the cloudless vault of the sky,
And sighing to the seething murmurs of the Ancient One-
Primordial Source of life wherein the winds were born.

A Wind,
Blowing across desolate waters
Skimmed by the tripping feet of sea birds
    winging over lonely oceans

O West Wind!
Dwelling in the abyss of the Dark Goddess;
You evoke the storm imprisoned in the bowl of night,
And, in the prodigious consummation
    of the passion of the gods,
You cast forth the hurricane
    into the trembling light world here above!
        Oh, divine and immortal rapture.
Translation from old Tuamotuan chant by J. Frank Stimson 1957

How the Polynesian used his winds and the average certainties of his weather
will be considered later on after we have given some attention to his navigation.

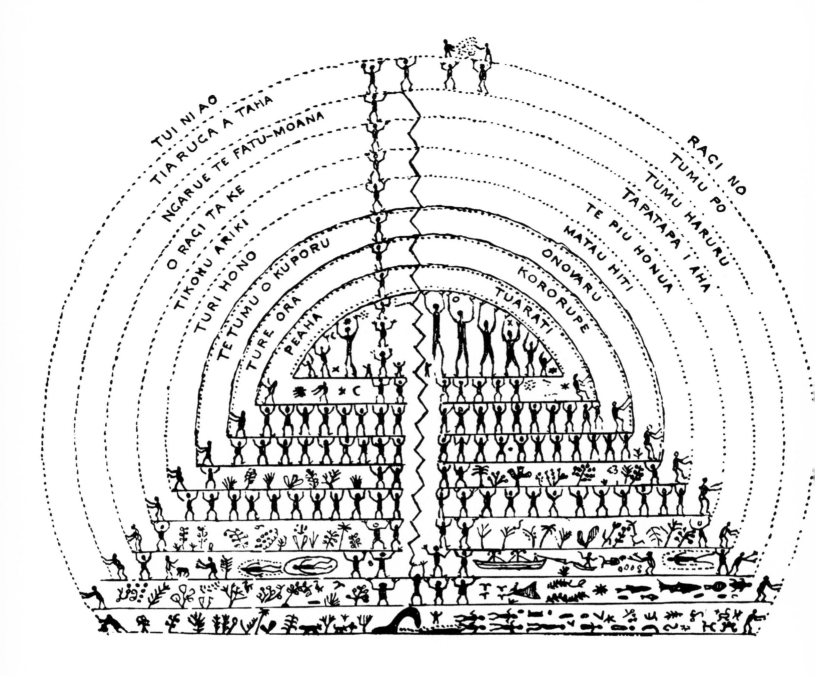

The Tuamotu Conception of the Heavens

This illustration was collected in 1869 by J. L. Young from Paiore, "an aged tuhunga
—wise man" who was a native of Anaa. He said that it was "the likeness of things made
known to the people of ancient times . . . and of the origin of things . . ." The lowest
division represents a period when the world was inhabited by animals not known to the
Islanders and when the sky hung low over the earth. In the ninth on the right side note
the constellation Scorpio and on the left, the moon and a star and a man making an offering. The canoes are those built by Rata, legendary nautical hero (see page 171), and the
double-masted one with its ladder tops and steering oar is easily recognized as the same
type depicted by Wilkes on page 111. Mr. Young feels that "the general idea is that of
ancient tradition: the raising of the heavens by human or rather superhuman effort."

Teuira Henry comments further on this drawing. "After the skies were disposed of, the
people, who were at that time immortal and endowed with great power, created the stars
to illuminate the highest heavens, the sun to shine lower down, and the moon nearest the
earth. All these celestial bodies rose up through shafts in their horizons in the east, and
set through others in corresponding horizons in the west, all in regular succession except
the sun, which caused the days and nights to be irregular. The hero Maui . . . regulated
the sun by seizing it by its rays . . . in the same way as described in other legends."

CELESTIAL NAVIGATION

An Art and a Science

Besides weather the other uncertainty that has plagued all of our Eurasian blue-water seafarers until the time of Cook is celestial navigation. For many years now I have been pondering the complexities and mysteries of Polynesian navigational systems. It is an old subject and many good men from Captain Cook to Harold Gatty have exercised their brains over it. So much concerning it has been written over, argued over, and fought over that you would think it might be an old rag wrung dry. But follow awhile and perhaps you may find something fresh and even exciting.

I have conscientiously studied the historical references and accounts. In this particular field the sources are well known and relatively few so that after ten years of assiduous poking about, a man becomes reasonably confident that he can say he has had a look at just about all of them. Contemporary references; that is, within the past fifty years; are more elusive. Those that appear in books are easy enough to check (and usually to toss out) as are those that appear in recognized special journals (not so tossable). Those that find their irrational ways to odd, upstart periodicals, one-shot publications or academic theses (most of them crackpot, but some few, inspired) can usually be accounted for only by lucky happenstance.

What seems the most striking generalization that one can make about all of these searchers into the Polynesian navigational mystery is that every one of them, unexceptionally, damns or praises the Polynesian in the terms of his own European concepts and gives little or no consideration to the obvious fact that the Polynesian was, and is, a different sort of fellow who cannot possibly be measured by the European yardstick.

We Europeans, over a long period of literacy, astronomy, geometry, chronology, have developed an intricate, accurate system of measurements; of angles, of distances, of time. Our most fundamental concept from a navigational viewpoint was latitude and longitude, theoretical grid lines projected upon the whole of the earth's surface. Everything can be pinpointed on this grid, but its actual existence lies only in our minds, for the imaginary grid must be transferred with graphic lines onto flat paper or a round globe before it can yield results. For the deep-sea navigator the only constants that can guide him about this world are the sun and stars; even they are inconstant, but from a practical view unimportantly so. So the Europeans set about to devise ways to find themselves, their islands and the features of their lands on this ingenious grid. The equator and the poles are understandable enough, but how the circumference came to be divided into 360° and how these degrees of arc and distance came to synchronize with units of time is a wonder that seems to have been foreordained by the nature of the universe rather than invented by man. The concept probably came from the thirty days of a moon and the twelve moons of a year. Socrates' "heaven" or "true earth" is a dodecahedron, a sphere of twelve pieces and, according to Plutarch, "seems to resemble both the Zodiac and the year, it being divided into the same number of pieces as these." The Oxford English Dictionary says that the "degree" is a very ancient concept originally applied to the circle of the zodiac; that is, the stage or distance traveled by the sun each day. It is of Babylonian and/or Egyptian origin based on sexagismal fractions first applied by Ptolemy about 150 A.D. The "hour" apparently did not come along until the 13th Century.

Over the centuries the Europeans measured their angles and timed their declinations with astrolabe, cross-staff, quadrant, and sextant. After much trial and much clever speculation, practical application evolved; latitude became ascertainable, longitude had to wait a few more centuries until mechanical technology made the chronometer sufficiently accurate. Meanwhile another much older technological discovery, the compass, handmaiden of magnetism, had come to be of significant value, supplemental and complemental to the whole geometrical, astronomical, temporal concept.

Our Scientific System

This method is essentially a combination of trigonometry and time. With his sextant the navigator measures the number of degrees in the angle between a star and the horizon. He does this by catching a double image of the star in the mirrors of his sextant and then carefully guiding one of these bright pinpoint reflections to the line of the horizon. When they coincide, he calls out "Mark!" to a shipmate who records the hour, minute, and second shown at that instant on the ship's chronometer. He then reads and records the degrees, minutes, and seconds of arc shown on the scale of his sextant. Then he takes aim at his next star.

All of this is a somewhat hazardous operation, for many variable conditions have to be met. In the first place the weather must be clear, although a familiar star can often be fetched out from scudding clouds. It can be performed only at dawn or dusk during the few minutes when stars are visible and the horizon line is sharp, just before the sun rises or just after it sets. The navigator must guide his reflected star while gripping with his feet a heaving and pitching deck, both of his hands being occupied with the sextant. The star he picks must be a sufficiently bright one and it must stand not too high above the horizon nor too low upon it, an angle of about 20° to 70°. If higher than that, its angle becomes unreliable; if lower, it becomes too narrow and atmospheric conditions approaching the horizon distort the accuracy. At least two stars must be used and laterally they must be at a serviceable angular distance apart; that is, not much more than 120°, nor much less than 45° so that they can be convincingly "crossed" at an angle that is neither too acute nor too obtuse. This requires some shrewd selecting, but after you have lived with your stars night after night it is not difficult, providing you are traveling at a sailing pace. Three or four stars are usually "shot," and sometimes the same ones are duplicated at different intervals if the navigator is clever and the twilight is lengthy enough.

The next step, of course, is to translate the ascension angles of the stars into lines on your chart, and where these lines intersect is your position at sea or "fix," as it is called. The translation of these degrees, minutes, and seconds of arc and of time into a line on the chart is a highly intricate mathematical process involving secants and cosecants, sines, cosines, and haversines, Greenwich mean time, and other technical mysteries that are comprehended by very few practicing navigators. But fortunately a mastery of mathematics is not necessary to the navigator because all of this work has been done for him and he needs only to consult the right tables and columns in his navigational manuals and *Nautical Almanac* and then add, divide, subtract a bit and the lines practically draw themselves.

Shooting the sun for noon latitudes and for morning and afternoon check positions on his dead-reckoning course is an important supplemental process for our "scientific" navigator, but for the Polynesian it is a concept that seems even more remote than our star sight system.

All of this was and is an elaborate, highly sophisticated edifice. It relies on such huge distances and such minute refinements that it seems impossible to the uninitiated that it could result in a workable method for a relatively uneducated and unsophisticated sea captain to find his way with reasonable certainty over two or three thousand miles of open sea to a small island or a particular port that is no more than a speck on his maritime chart. But only the simple bones have been listed; hour angles, declinations, right ascensions, parallax and refraction, and many other such abstrusities must be reckoned with, all of them hinging on the interrelated concept of degrees, minutes, and seconds of arc, of time, of distance. Besides these, there are vagaries of the compass; variation and deviation and local magnetic adjustments. It is all almost incredible, but it does work; moreover, a simple man by simple rote can master it.

* * *

"The ability to establish a line of position by observation of a celestial body is based on the fundamental fact that, for any given instant of time, the altitude and azimuth of a celestial body in relation to the horizon of any assumed position of latitude can be calculated using formulas and tables made available to the mariner by the astronomer. This is the basis of *all celestial navigation.*"*—from *Navigation and Nautical Astronomy,* the standard textbook for this subject at the U.S. Naval Academy at Annapolis, original edition 1926 by Commander Benjamin Dutton.

* * *

Can you, who know our friends down under, conceive of translating this admirably succinct credo for the edification of an old-time *tahuna* who has just brought his canoe a thousand miles or so from Manua to Raiatea? One is tempted to repeat again the account of the master of the *Morning Star* in 1860 who greeted a Micronesian canoe-load of some forty persons when they glided alongside him in the harbor of a mid-Pacific atoll after a straight-as-a-string, open-ocean voyage of several hundred miles and came aboard for a cigarette. He was astonished at their accomplishment and his first reaction (of course) was to show their captain how his own compass operated. The Polynesian captain professed, obligingly, to be impressed, but when the demonstration was concluded, he waved his hand casually toward a shaggy-haired companion squatting in the scuppers and said, "His head all same your compass."

*Italics mine.

Yes, consider the Polynesian. He did not write; he did not figure; he had no instruments, no maps or charts, no compass. The prevalent conclusion of impossible is understandable enough. Yet there he was, long before our navigators even dreamed of getting there, on ocean islands thousands of miles over the open sea while we had not settled larger islands only a few hundred miles off our Atlantic coasts.

So the next step is to try to figure out how this "primitive" could have done it. Let us dismiss the accidental-voyage theory; that is too easy an explanation and by now it is rather conclusively dismissed by all except its hardy "originator." First the "primitive" is conceded a rough latitude. Polaris in the Hawaiian neighborhood and Crux in the south will allow him to estimate that. Then steer by the rising or setting stars; they are, again roughly, equivalent to a crude compass. Waves and winds and swells and rips; driftwood, seaweed and birds; clouds stopped by peaks or reflecting lagoons; smells of lands and sounds of reefs; all of these and other such are conceded to him and he is granted a superhuman sensitivity of them.

That fairly sums up, I think, the concessions that the usual European navigational expert is willing to bestow upon the Polynesian navigator. There are only two voices missing, two of real consequence; that of Harold Gatty and his zenith star theory and that of David Lewis and his experimental voyage. Now we are getting closer; this is new ground, thinking the Polynesian way. But not close enough. What if he is blown off course by a two- or three-day storm? How about cross currents? And leeward drift? These are inescapable hazards to precise or even adequately certain navigation. The most dedicated Polynesiac cannot explain them away. Andrew Sharp uses them again and again to obliterate his opponents.

No, we must have a look at this mystery from another perspective. We must cease trying to figure how close the Polynesian came to our navigational system, especially of how he might approximate latitude and guess at longitude. We must seek out an entirely different system, a basic, comprehensive one that is conceived in his terms as a Polynesian, not in ours as a European.

Harold Gatty, after circumnavigating the globe as an airplane pilot, began to do that during the war when he was searching for a noninstrumental way for a man lost at sea. His insight and intuition developed the zenith star theory which picks out for each island a particular star that, spotted at its zenith, will guide you to that island and that one alone. This is a refreshingly non-European concept that puts us on a new track. It has great merit, but he expected too much of it; it is not a system, only a part of one. And even Gatty himself envisioned it only as a means of determining latitude. (He also suggests a broken oar held at arm's length to measure, like the old-time cross-staff, a rough angle of latitude and an extended arm with outspread thumb and fingers to measure degrees to the right or left of guiding stars.)

But the Polynesian had no angles or degrees; he did not think that way. What we must do is to throw overboard the whole notion of a latitude and longitude grid. It is patently non-Polynesian. The Polynesian never thinks in terms of lines and abstract intervals of measure. His inches, feet, and yards, his whole linear system is resolved in the breadth of the hand, the digital span, the divided forearm, the finger tip to elbow, to shoulder; the outstretched arms to make his fathom; the up or down elevation of his palm to show height. Distances overland or up the mountain or across the sea he measures by the time it takes to negotiate them.

Especially he does not think in terms of arbitrarily placed and spaced lines that must be expressed in graphic markings on flat paper. He makes almost no graphic representations of any sort, not even in his art. Even less, of course, does he conceive of a round globe with parallels rising and falling one way while meridians converge and disperse in another. He does not place his islands by their relative positions north and south, east and west. He places them in the direction where they lie from where he is standing. Gatty says they had "no word for distance, no use for space."

If we are sitting at *Vaima* in Papeete sipping a Hinano beer and I am telling you of my recent voyage on the copra boat *Taporo* to the Marquesas, you may ask me where the Marquesas are. I will get out a sheet of paper and a pencil to draw you a rough map. You understand immediately. Our Tahitian companion will not. He will simply thrust his arm out, palm-flat, fingers-closed, hand-vertical, toward Point Venus; the direction of the Marquesas from where we are. If you ask him how far it is, he will say two days and two nights on the *Taporo*.

This instinctive rejection of graphics vitiates star angles and sun angles of all sorts, except that the Polynesian obviously knew well how high the celestial pole rose on his island and on those of his familiar neighbors, near or far. He knew also where the sun at all its wanderings from solstice to solstice belonged in his sky. This rejection of angles gives the deep-six forever to the notorious "sacred calabash." No one who ever knew a Polynesian could ever have put any credence in such a contraption or in the weird fancies of Michener. It explains perhaps why the only "charts" the Polynesian did invent, the Micronesian swell and current guides, were not constructed to scale. Perhaps it even takes with it also the concept of the star compass and the sixteen point wind rose.

So abolish all this marvelous, theoretical structure that has served us so well and what have you to go on?

Surprisingly you have quite a lot, but the first way, perhaps the only way, certainly the best way to assess it is to go to the South Seas and have a look at the Polynesian and his habits. Firstly you will notice that he tends to travel by night. That is when his senses are sharpest and his energies most unfailing. Our day goes from midday to midday, with midnight marking the half way. This in itself is now an abstraction when you come to think of it; no one without a sextant's mirrors to his eye knows when the sun hits the meridian and only the clock tells you midnight. The seagoing Polynesian's "day" goes from starrise to starrise with the half way marked by starset or sunrise. Or you might say that his "day" begins at sunset. Old-time reports and modern instincts, including most importantly the moon which was his best short-term nondiurnal clock (as it is ours and especially our women's), indicate that he reckoned his intervals from night to night rather than, as we do, from day to day. Certainly his year began with the first appearance in the evening twilight of *matariki*, the Pleiades, toward the end of our November, just as our sidereal year begins with the first point of Aries. Abraham Fornander who was one of the earliest and most voluminous recorders of Hawaiian lore and custom says, "The Polynesians counted time by the nights - *Po*. 'Tomorrow' was *A-po-po*, lit. the night's night. 'Yesterday' was *Po-i-nehe-nei*, the past night . . . This method of reckoning by nights ascends to the hoariest antiquity."

At sea the day was of relatively little use. Our old-time, hard-shell sea captains invariably concede the Polynesian a noon latitude and easy steering "by the sun."

To our sea captains the noon latitude is easy; they learn how to measure its angle in high school. To the Polynesian it was incomprehensible and therefore useless. To a sea captain a star is useful only for a few minutes before sunrise or after sunset when he can get a sharp horizon line in his sextant mirrors. To the Polynesian a star was of value all night long *between* these intervals, not *at* them. As a guiding star each one was useful only while near the horizon, but others kept rising out of the same "pit" or setting into it. The Polynesian was and still is as much a nocturnal as a diurnal animal, especially at sea. He probably did most of his paddling at night and slept during the day when he was not protected as he was on land by trees and shadows from the merciless sun.

This is an important adjustment for you to make when you first arrive in Polynesia. Your next most pragmatic line of action is to go lie flat on the top of the cabin of a small boat and have a look at the night sky. A hard flat deck is recommended, with no more than a tarpaulin under you and a couple of meters of pareu cloth over you; no pillow, you want to look as close to 180° from your feet as you can arch your neck. A hilltop will do or a coral beach if you can find one that is not screened by coconut trees. The hard deck is recommended because your bones, if they are as old as those of some of us, will ache from its rigors to wake you every quarter or half hour and persuade you, no matter how sleepy, to shift from left side to back or from backside to right and over again. These successive shifts will give you periodical looks at the stars all through the night and thus a splendid idea of their majestic movement. If you are in the month of May and you arch your head northward, you will see the Great Dipper stretched flat over the horizon pouring its contents below. Look down askance through the back of your skull and you see or imagine Polaris at the celestial north pole. Then look up over your toes and there plainly is the conical void of the southern pole well designated by the pointers of the Cross and the three tail stars of the Scorpion with more distant bearings from Orion and Pegasus. To your right sprawls Orion settling in the west; to your left Scorpius is soaring out of the east.

After a few hours those waking intervals blend and you are conscious of great, sweeping, star paths crossing the sky. Think of the inside of your head as a camera on time exposure recording a giant grid. There are many stars; so many that you might expect to be confused, but they do not bewilder; they fall into recognized patterns. Even the lesser ones maintain an easy individuality. After a while you feel not only familiar with this great wheeling display but you feel at home in it. You come to think you know precisely where you are, for the whole vast, intricate web seems to radiate from a pinpoint in your minute skull upon your tiny island in a small area of the Pacific, itself only a spot in an ocean huge to you but no larger to those stars than the speck on the European navigator's chart.

It is a curious sensation, this feeling that you know where you are in that whole brilliant maze and that the entire dome is swiveled precisely on you. But it is a real sensation and one that recurs night after night. It can come to you only as you lie on your island in the sea; no such fixed sensation could occur on a moving vessel. It may seem presumptuous to imagine that you can pinpoint yourself amongst the stars, even foolishly egocentric, but it happens; it persists and I believe it is not too difficult to explain. I believe, too, that it had a lot to do with the Polynesian's ability to navigate.

By way of explanation; first off it gives you the idea of star paths rather than star points or star angles. These paths arch up from horizon east, transcribe their ways across the firmanent and slide down under horizon west. One of them, only one path as Gatty points out, goes directly over your head on your particular island. That is your zenith star or stars-in-line. The many, many others sweep up and away in all of their appointed, invariable tracks, from many starting points along the eastern rim to many disappearing points along the western rim. These tracks when you know them give you a multitude of related bearings to tell you where you are. These are not latitudes and longitudes that go at right angles east and west, north and south. These are great arcs of light like bars of a celestial cage that, as you move about within it, show you from many related directions and many graded heights just where you are. From the sky patterns above, if you know them well enough, you know your place beneath.

It is dangerous indeed to relate animal instincts or genetically determined mechanisms to human behavior. Yet it is tempting to call attention here to the discoveries of Franz Sauer and his wife at the University of Freiburg in the late 1950s. By ingenious experiments with European warblers they have demonstrated that these birds are guided by particular star patterns which they can recognize and to which they can orient themselves even under laboratory conditions when they have never seen a star until maturity. Obviously this is not to say that the Polynesians had star-guided instincts, but does it not at least argue that if specific star patterns are significantly recognizable even to birds and are used by them for consistent celestial navigation, that such star patterns could be recognized and used by men for the same purpose? And this, mind you, without benefit of a latitude/longitude concept or even the crudest astrolabe.

Of course if you are navigating at sea instead of lying on an island shore, you are concerned firstly and always with one primary series of positions; the path that goes from the island you are leaving to the island that you are headed for. That is your course; you must always stay on that path or get back to it if winds or currents carry you to one side or another. All the other arching star paths in the sky are to be related to that primary series. These and these alone will get you to your goal. As you move along, the others will, however, help to tell you how far along you are, when you are there or supposed to be there, and then, perhaps, they will tell you if you have overshot your mark.

We use a magnetic compass for our primary bearing path, but even that marvel of natural technology is of little help when you are unknowingly carried off course, unless and until it can be set aright by latitude and longitude sights from sun and stars. In other words the compass does not point out a constant course from departure island to destination island; it tells you only where to go from where you are. All this, even determining the compass course in the first place, is predicated on transferring everything to a paper chart. How then did the Polynesian find that essential primary and constant bearing path and most importantly, how did he stick to it?

The answer at first appears to be simple; so simple that it seems strange that only the Polynesian has hit upon it before; strange, that is, until you realize that he, and only he, in his latitudes could make use of it. This method is not new to us; it has been noted by students of Polynesia and recorded by their historians, but its significance and especially its practical application seem not to have been fully appreciated as yet. The missionary, John Williams, in 1837 gives us the first clue.

*   *   *

"We had still one more island to seek; and, finding Roma-tane exceedingly intelligent, we inquired of him if he had ever heard of Rarotonga; 'Oh yes!' he replied, 'it is only a day and a night's sail from Atiu, we know the way there.' This information delighted us, but when we inquired of him the position in which it lay, he at one time pointed in one direction, and another in quite the opposite. But this was soon explained; for the natives, in making their voyages, do not leave from any part of an island, as we do, but, invariably, have what may be called starting-points. At these places they have certain land-marks, by which they steer, until the stars become visible; and they generally contrive to set sail so as to get sight of their heavenly guides by the time their land-marks disappear. Knowing this, we determined to adopt the native plan, and steered our vessel round to the 'starting-point.' Having arrived there, the chief was desired to look to the land-marks, while the vessel was being turned gradually round; and when his marks on the shore ranged with each other, he cried out, 'That's it! that is it!' I looked immediately at the compass, and found the course to be S.W. by W.; and it proved to be as correct as if he had been an accomplished navigator. I mention this circumstance, because I think it to be of universal importance to all persons, in every scientific or other expedition, who seek information from natives, as it shows the correctness of their knowledge; but they must be allowed to communicate it in their own particular way. . . . So it was with us; and, had we not adopted the method we did, Rarotonga, in all probability, would have been unblessed with the knowledge of salvation to the present day."

*   *   *

He thus resolves his confusion by postulating the theory of "starting points" or "land-marks, by which they steer," a theory that has recently been expounded in careful (though unconvincing) detail by Captain Hilder in *Polynesian Navigation.* I believe that they may frequently have used land ranges when setting out in the daytime, but that these were indications of their forthcoming star path not pointers for a whole voyage as Captain Hilder thinks. This would give them a headstart in daylight when it is more convenient to negotiate a pass through the reef, to secure for sea, and to get clear of nearby islands. Captain Hilder's puzzlement at the rarity of his guide stones could be explained if natural ranges (configurations of the land), rather than man-made markers, were used and this seems more likely, especially for volcanic islands.

In the same publication a quotation from Maud Makemson outlines the general idea but does not seem to realize the vital use of it. In his scholarly and wide-ranging summary of the migration of the ocean peoples, Professor G. S. Parsonson refers to Makemson and others and seems to take a usable system pretty much for granted, as if others had solved it so he need not delve too closely into the details. "That the system was effective cannot be doubted. It could hardly otherwise have been invented. But it may be suspected that . . . it was particularly suited to shorter distances . . . Its defects are obvious enough," etc. Makemson in her own book, *The Morning Star Rises* comes closer, but good astronomer as she is, it is evident from many things she says and leaves unsaid that she is not much of a navigator. "When night fell the ship was again aligned between two stars in the same declinations and having the same diurnal paths as the bow and stern stars of the early morning . . . However since they had no means of determining their position at sea, and in view of the fact that their method of navigation did not permit them to correct for lateral drift, they found it advisable to wait for a wind from astern when they wished to set a direct course to a distant island." And she illustrates her deduction with a diagram that shows a ship on a southerly bearing, indicating that she is not aware of great circle complications.

The early German anthropologist, Augustin Kramer, came closest when he wrote: "So they searched for a setting star which sets in the same latitude and at the same time at which Orion rises, as, for instance, Arcturus in Boötes. If one aligned astern to the setting star and one aligned ahead to the rising star and the ship then stood not in line, they could guess easily if they had gone too far north or too far south off of this course line. This steering ahead and astern at the same time was one of the artful skills of the old navigators."

But he has previously said, "My old friend L'eiato of Tutuila went to much trouble to explain this kind of navigation to me, and once when he had come one evening for this purpose, but could not finish his lecture because some stars were missing . . . he did not let me go until sunrise. I have to acknowledge that I did not understand everything . . . because I am too bad an astronomer and also the whole matter seemed to me not very simple."

Gatty, to whom this method's virtues would seem most significant, is so absorbed in his zenith star discovery that he feels that it alone is sufficient and seems to be unaware of the existence of this old Polynesian way. Two contemporary scientists, Goodenough and Frankel, postulate a "star compass" but do not convey convincing ideas of its practical use and make no reference to fore-and-aft stars. David Lewis refers to his "Ara whetu," his "star path," with certain stars ahead and certain others astern, but he seems to use this ara as one would use a compass to readjust his course when he finds it in error or sufficiently suspects it to be so. He changes his star path to fit the new situation; he does not hasten back to his initial and always dependable constant path as, I believe, the Polynesian did. He writes: "The 'star path' of course only indicated the direction of the star [toward which they were headed] much as a compass would." But since his double-hulled yacht was sailing from Tahiti to New Zealand, a fore-and-aft system would have only limited usefulness for him.

A compass course can only lead you from where you are to where you are going; that is its limitation because you are always wandering, at least to some extent, at the mercy of currents, storms, and leeway. A fore-and-aft star course, on the other hand, is a firm constant; its only limitation is your capacity to know its intricacies and subtleties. To steer by a star or steer by a compass, as any good sailor knows, is a toss-up. There are fluctuations aplenty in both, but the errors tend to equalize themselves in a reassuring way.

And thus we have found hints and clues and feelers from Williams in 1837 and Kramer in 1901 to Beaglehole off Puka Puka in 1938, and on to Makemson in 1941, Gatty in 1943, Frankel in 1962, Hilder in 1963, Lewis in 1966. These are by no means all who contributed; they are the ones who seem to me most significant. Sharp (1956) is obviously oblivious because over and over in varied phraseology he says, "Horizon stars give no clue whatever to lateral deviation." This is always his clincher. Can we slip it with a sharp jerk as we would a granny knot? Perhaps we can under certain important circumstances though not under others.

47

The Fore-and-Aft
Star System

When the early Polynesian in his equatorial latitudes set out from island A to island B, he steered for the star that rose (or fell) on the horizon in the exact location of B from A. He knew that particular star, let us call it star X, from long observation and time-old familiarity. He knew equally well another star falling on the precise opposite side of the heavens, 180° in our terms, or directly to the rear of the course he was steering. Let us call this one star Y. In other words while

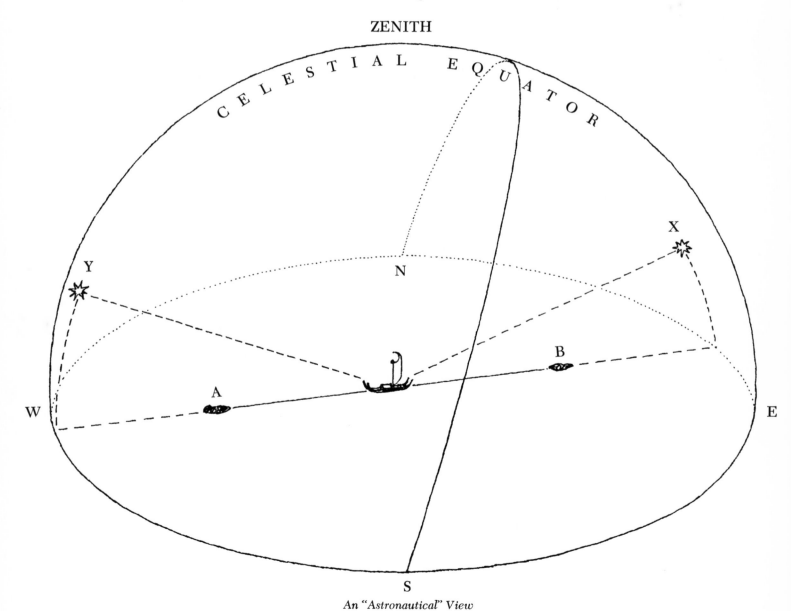

An "Astronautical" View

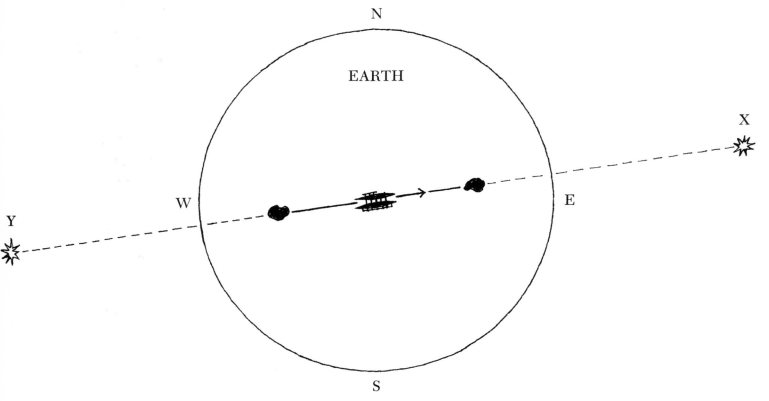

A View from the Zenith Directly Above

star X appeared in the direction of his goal, island B, star Y would at the same time always be present in the direction of his departure island, A. All he needed to do was to stand in the middle of his canoe, sight his goal star over his bow and his departure star over his stern. If they lined up, he could be nowhere except on his direct course. If he was carried to one side or another by storm or current or lee-way, he had only to take his 180° bearing or azimuth and then scramble back to his primary bearing path by sail or paddle. Once back on it, he could safely resume his journey.

Our navigational proclivities always start from where we are and concentrate on where we are going. At sea the spot where we are is always moving and thus must be refound or repositioned at every practical interval and our course read-justed to where we are going. This is an intricate procedure, but we have worked it out over many centuries and it is now virtually computerized for us (or by us). The Polynesian concept was very much more simple; it was based on four fixed points: two stars fore and aft, two islands on the straight line between them. The movable point, our canoe, need only worry about its progress along that line. Our European system in comparison is based on one self-centered point, our canoe, which wanders about our suppositioned grid in all directions. But it can always be located by star or sun sights even after a blind interval and then redirected toward its objective by compass. The Polynesian needed only to get back on his pre-determined and constant line and keep going.

Like most simple things, his constant line had difficulties. It was not always easy to find or to stick to. No two stars will last you through the night; only a part of it. Then you must pick up a couple of others, and they do not always line up just where you want them. So you must make careful allowances, aligning to the right of one and to the left of another with varying intervals to be learned in order to keep to your proper path.

The Polynesian had an ingenious way of reconciling these offsets of stars from his path. We steer by a star and the habit is so ingrained in us that it has seemed clearer to propound a fore-and-aft "star" course. Actually the Polynesian aimed for a "pit," on (or below) the rim of the horizon, from which his star, or rather his procession of stars emerged; and also the "pit" on the opposite horizon into which they fell. Thus we ought really to call this theory the fore-and-aft *pit* system.

All this may seem a quibble at first glance, but from a practical steersman's point of view, it is an important concept to keep in mind. The pit lies right on the horizon; it does not move up into the sky as the star does. The star above becomes merely an indicator of the course mark below. And most importantly when one star soars too high or too obliquely, another pops up to mark the same point. And if there is not another nicely in line, there are a couple that indicate the pit between them. Speed this action up as you would a movie camera and you have a font of stars spouting out of your pit all night long; and, of course, a cascade, 180° away, disappearing into your complementary pit. This concept once visualized, memorized, and practised at sea is much more reliable than trying to remember to head to the north of one star and to the south of another. Moreover, it is a genuine Polynesian concept for it occurs again and again in old myths and legends, and there are still Pacific islanders today who use the same expression.

One should also remember that however subsequent stars might vary from side to side, the Polynesian could always get a positive fix on his course every clear night with his two original or most accurate stars, at least. A fix every twenty-four hours is a navigator's definition of heaven. Kjell Akerblom believes that at least eight and preferably nine stars would have been necessary to guide the steersman the night through. By the fore-and-aft method this would mean sixteen to eighteen stars, which is certainly asking a lot; not only a lot, but far more than necessary. It makes me wonder if Akerblom has done much sailing by stars at night.

While horizon stars were rising and falling fore and aft and had to be changed as they rose too high or sank too low, the Polynesian navigator had another cleverly conceived recourse to keep him on his predetermined path. Kramer reports it, a bit clumsily perhaps, but enough to give us a valuable clue. "If horizon or meridian stars were absent, they still had another method of their own. They would search for any combination of three stars in a line . . . Then one of the navigators would lay himself on his back in the narrow waist of the canoe, lengthwise, of course, and if he now saw the stars right above him in one line [that is, corresponding to the course of the boat as determined by horizon stars] . . . he could give directions to the steersman . . . and who watches the sky can see for himself that one can find many of these constellations of three especially in the southern milky way." And thus he had a huge celestial compass needle high above him that he could align with the small compass needle that was his canoe upon the surface of the sea. And if the comparison may be pursued even farther in spite of

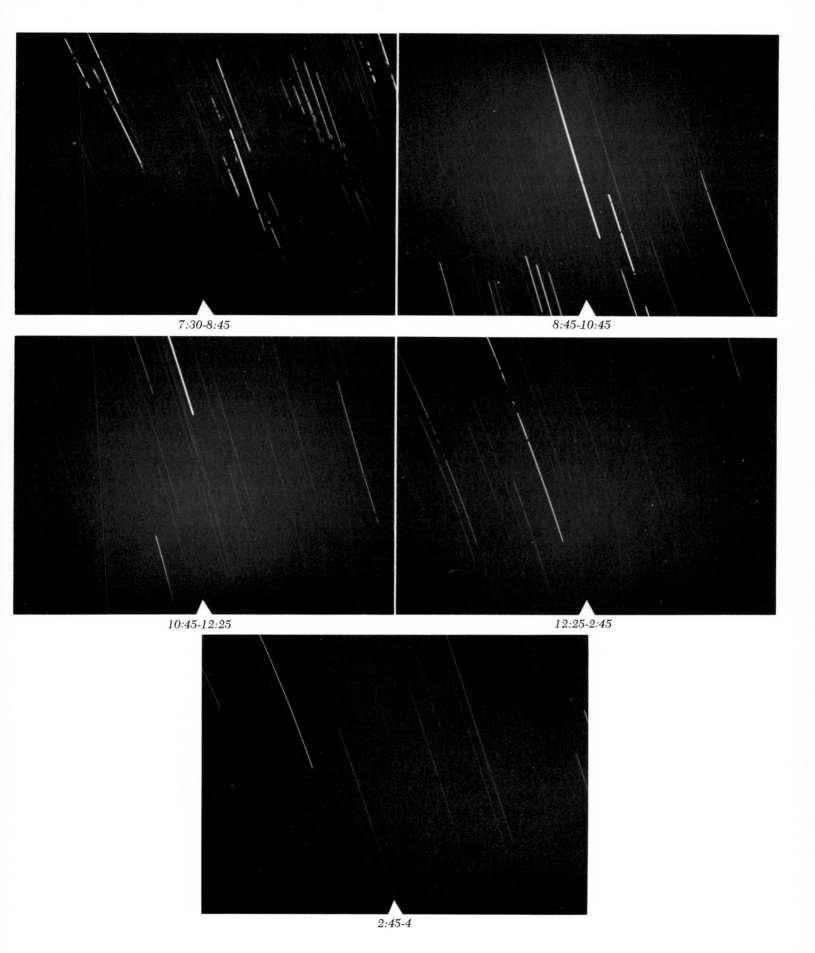

7:30-8:45

8:45-10:45

10:45-12:25

12:25-2:45

2:45-4

Star Paths and Star Pits

These photographs were taken on the edge of the lagoon at the southern tip of Raiatea pointing ENE to the southern shore of Huahine. The camera remained stationary, focused just above the horizon as would the eye of a navigator in a canoe and the frames of the film were changed at the intervals indicated. The first exposure is jiggly because too many people were curious during the first hour, but to a canoeist that might simulate a choppy sea. The "nick" in each picture represents the steering "pit."

the fact that, unlike our compass, it had nothing to do with magnetism, something might be visualized perhaps as useful as the little duplicate compass by which Captain Cook and other skippers of his time checked on their helmsmen on deck while lying in their bunks below by watching the little "telltale" hanging from their cabin ceiling.

Of course this whole system was vulnerable to weather, but no more so than ours at comparable eras. Another variable was seasonal change; the stars rise four minutes earlier each night, so the Polynesian must have known his sequence of moons from the beginning of the sidereal year with the first appearance of the *matariki* or Pleiades. He had to keep his calendar in his head, just as we keep the same sort of data in record books. But fortunately his head was roomy and accurate; the early missionaries and discoverers always marveled that he could predict the very night each year when the palolo worm would appear. It was a subtle calculation somewhat akin to our Easter, a moveable feast.

*   *   *

"The Matariki were originally one (star). Its bright effulgence excited the anger of the god Tane, who got hold of Aldebaran (Aumea) and Sirius (Mere), and chased the offender. The affrighted fugitive ran for his life, and took refuge behind a stream. But Sirius drained off the waters, thus enabling Tane to renew the chase. Finally, Tane hurled Aldebaran bodily against the exhausted fugitive, who was thereby splintered into six shining fragments. This cluster of little stars is appropriately named Mata-riki, or *little-eyes*, on account of their brightness. It is also designated Tau-Ono, or the *the-six*, on account of the apparent number of the fragments; the presence of the seventh star not having been detected by the unassisted native eye.

"Reinga thus sings of the wars of the star gods:

Ua riri paa Vena ra ia Aumea	Vena° was enraged against Aumea, (Aldebaran)
Noa kite ake i te kakenga	On account of the brillance of his rising.
Noa ui atu i te ara i pao ai Matariki ma	She demanded if he recollected the fate of the Pleiades,
E Mere ma e!	Shivered by Sirius and his friends.
Tuarangi maiti! Tuarangi maiti!	Alas! ye bright-shining gods! Bright-shining gods!"

An old Mangaian myth recorded by W. W. Gill, 1891

*   *   *

There is reason to believe that the Polynesians knew their stars to a degree that few other people have achieved. But all of the ancients were far more intimate with their heavens than the historical peoples have been until very recent scientific times, so comparisons have little merit. The Polynesian's knowledge, coming so recently into history, appears to be particularly impressive perhaps because his star names were recorded before they were forgotten. They had individual names for about two hundred stars which seems an astonishing number, but they recognized and used many more than that as associates of the named stars. That they were aware of such celestial goings-on as the solstices is evidenced by markings on the great trilithon, Ha'amonga, in Tonga and by the alignments of some

°Vena was a goddess, represented by the star, Procyon.

of the huge stone statues on Easter Island. Kenneth Emory writes that he does "not believe the ancient Polynesians possessed any sophisticated knowledge of astronomy. A few of the maraes of Polynesia and *ahu* of Easter Island may have been more or less purposely oriented in relation to the sun . . . Very likely some of the sages were quite aware of the northern and southern limits of the sun and fixed them through natural or artificial boundaries. But nothing at all, of course, like Stonehenge."

Memorizing the myriads of details was understandably enough a specialized art, just as was the memorizing of the long intricate genealogies. For such purposes specialists were not only trained but inherited, born, and raised: the *tahuna*, the wise man. Priest and artist were one and the same in Polynesia. The word that designated them both was *Tahuna* (with its dialectic variations, *Tufunga*: Samoa and Tonga, *Tau'a*: Tahiti, *Ta'unga*: Rarotonga, *Tohunga*: Maori, *Tahuna*: Marquesas, *Taura*: Mangareva, *Kahuna*: Hawaii, etc.) This title was bestowed on a Master or *Maestro* whatever his specialty and is translated in many ways by missionaries, traders, colonizers and anthropologists, each of whom gives the word his own preferred slant, though all translations bear the stamp of leadership: Priest, Seer, Author, Artist, Wise Man, Master Craftsman.

Translations that are conspicuous by their absence are Medicine Man, Magician, Shaman, the usual epithets for the man of magical influence in other precolonial societies. Even from the most bigoted early missionaries, the *Tahuna* commanded respect.

To the Polynesian himself the status of the *tahuna* was much the same as chief. Hereditary chiefs, *Arii*, were by blood the highest of all, though in some cases the "talking" chiefs who orated for them were more influential and not infrequently hereditary chiefs became so untouchable that they were mere figureheads. Thus they were philosophers, bishops, artists, scientists with many overlappings amongst them. Each was preeminent in his field. There were many of them, *tahuna* of the *marae* or temple, canoe builder, house builder, master fisherman, master of crops, doctor of medicine, artist, master of *tatu*, master of mnemonics, prophet and so on, but one of the most important and most highly specialized was the navigator who was an astronomer, sage of the winds, storms, stars; predictor of hurricanes, keeper of "knowledge of the earth's configurations." As in all societies these "priests" of navigation kept their knowledge to themselves and directed it to their heirs. Perhaps it was too abstruse or too detailed to share; perhaps they were jealous of their powers and prerogatives and wished to control the line of their successions. In any case we can see the sort of ingrained complusions to secrecy at work here that plague our specialists today and perhaps explain why the Polynesian's marvelous navigational arts have been elusive mysteries to us.

The navigational stars listed in our Nautical Almanac *are 57 for every hour of every day in the year and for every place on earth. The Polynesians knew the names of 200 stars for their region of the equatorial Pacific alone.*

But...

and this is a very big but; such a system could only work with reasonable dependability when going east or west not far from the equator. Any fore-and-aft star course is a so-called "great circle" course; that is, you are steering by points at infinite distances out in space. When sailing east or west near enough to the equator, this will not affect the lineup of your stars. But if you are sailing north or south, lateral winds and currents could carry you off course halfway round the world and your fore-and-aft stars would line up just the same.

This is not an easy concept to understand, but it is crucial to this whole argument. Consider your two points to be Polaris ahead, the pit of Crux behind; you are sailing over the surface of a globe with an imaginary line running through its middle reaching out a few trillion miles ahead to one pinpoint of light and another few trillion to a pit point of darkness behind you. The points where the ends of the line lead may be two excellent bearings, but the globe, alas, is rotating at a steady pace and those points will direct your course equally well whether you are on the top of globe or on the bottom; it makes no difference to them way out there in space. But it makes a whale of a difference to you sailing on the globe. Indeed it rules out at least half of your precious system. But fortunately for the early Polynesian, the part that remains is the part that he needed; for his islands were near the equator and when he went exploring, he headed east for his bow star until he either found a new island or reached his point of no return. Then he came back westward on his stern star. And for his course it mattered not that the earth was rotating beneath him because he was interested only in courses that paralleled or coincided with its rotation. Moreover his "pit" method fixed the point toward which he was always steering on the horizon and, because of the curvature of the earth, the horizon to a man standing in a canoe is only a few miles away. Thus in a sense he brought those infinitely distant stars down to earth.

This fore-and-aft star method seems almost absurdly simple and it is simple in theory. In practice, although it required no special skill, it did demand a very considerable knowledge and experience of the heavens. Its success in its larger aspects was and is dependent upon a virtual memorization of the useful stars for each course and their seasonal habits. It was not necessary to use the brightest stars; the weaker ones were often more effective and could be easily identified in relation to each other. With this in mind it becomes evident that the knowledgeable Polynesian *tahuna* had a huge selection at his disposal. Lest such a multitude strain your belief in even a Polynesian memory, remember that any one *tahuna* did not need to keep voyages of all directions in his head; each navigator might specialize on only one or two or three objectives, and those only in certain set seasons.

*   *   *

". . . every master and pilot prided himself on knowing exactly how much way his ship was making. He knew the ship, he considered the wind, he watched the sails, he watched the water. In fact, it was a matter which just could not be explained to the landsman. A good sailor knew his ship, and that was all."

—E. G. R. Taylor, writing of thirteenth-century sea captains

*   *   *

In general, this kind of navigation is the sort that leads from one particular place to another particular place somewhat as a blazed tree trail led the American Indian through the woods from one camp ground to another or as a known star route leads the Bedouin over the desert from one oasis to another. It is not a system, like our celestial navigation, that enables you to go wherever you wish to wander, adjusting your course to variables of weather or even as the old Nantucketers did, adjusting to the whims of whales. A set of particular fore-and-aft stars or series of stars could be fairly easily memorized for individual journeys. A man need only watch them night after night go by his island toward where he knew his destination lay. Cross bearing stars, zenith stars, and grid patterns to position the progress of those journeys was a more taxing challenge, especially for long hauls, and could be achieved only by experience. But even on the longest of these, the fore-and-aft system must have been well-nigh infallible once it was fully mastered. Indeed, when you grasp it clearly and make allowance for its geographical limitations, it seems more foolproof and much less complex in operation than our compass and celestial sight method.

Exploratory Voyaging

And so assuming that one of the prime uncertainties, navigation, can be coped with to a reasonable degree, we can take a somewhat different view of the motivations of the early Polynesian seafarers and of how they were related to and conditioned by their weather. Of their descendents who went north to Hawaii and south to New Zealand, we will concern ourselves later on. Their problems, both of weather and of navigation, were quite different and therefore required different solutions.

First off, granting the early Polynesian can without too much difficulty find his way by the stars eastward or westward as he wants, why does he want to? Secondly, how does he discover or determine these so valuable star courses before he sets out to where they lead him? Even with navigational skills well developed, it is still a long, hard pull from Samoa to Raiatea and even from Tahiti to Nuku Hiva. (1) Adventure? I doubt it. He can be presumed to be adventurous; most people are, though some more so than others. This is an important component, but only to incurable romantics is it a primary driving force. (2) Exploration? He must, of course, know where he is going before he can deliberately go any-where, so exploration is a first necessary step, but that makes it a secondary mo-tivation. (3) Conquest? There we have it; conquest is the basic drive once the population pressures have built up and voyaging is in the air. Whether to con-quer virgin land or to conquer other people; in either case (4) colonization is a subsequent subsidiary motivation and (5) escape is an appendicidal one, once he had started on his long trek from the Asian mainland.

Harry Payne Whitney's concept that migration made its way *against* the winds rather than *with* them gives us a whole new slant on Polynesian voyaging. His theory would not be as convincing without the assumption of the fore-and-aft star path navigational method, but with a set of reciprocal courses at our disposal we can perhaps make a good case for deliberate voyaging leading to settlement in sequential steps.

In the first place let us understand that this would probably be done against the trades in the finest, most dependable weather, the general idea being to go out looking for unknown land the hardest way in order to come back safely the easiest way. Sailing into the unknown with women and pigs aboard to find an island has always seemed to me a foolhardy business no matter how intrepid and adven-turesome the Polynesian might be. And a constant stream of such reckless voyages would have to be assumed if one takes accidental settlement seriously. As Whit-ney points out, such a policy is just not sound seamanship, and the Polynesian was a sound seaman. Sound seamanship, especially when exploring for an unknown objective means taking the fewest possible risks of not getting home safely. You are willing to take plenty of chances on the way out in order to be as sure as you can be that on the way back the dangers will be minimal. You would go as far as you could until your food supply told you it was time to head back home.

So the Polynesian planned his migratory movements in several stages. Let us suppose that a certain chief and his tribe have lived for many generations in the Samoan islands and in the years ahead he foresees the desirability of finding new land for himself and his people. Perhaps population pressures have built up on his present island and he realizes that it is only a matter of time before his more powerful neighbor will want to make war and drive him out. Perhaps he is the younger son of a paramount chief and he knows that his older brother will inherit the title and the land. He may be ambitious and adventurous and want a chiefdom for himself. Perhaps family blood lines forbid the girl he loves and his only recourse is to abduct her and set up housekeeping on another island. Perhaps recurrent famines caused by droughts in his windward valley make him long for more fertile prospects. And so on . . . whatever the underlying impulses or combination of them, he decides to go exploring. He has time enough and enough resources. He is not going to build a canoe and sail precipitately into nowhere as is the popular assumption of the accidentalists. He wants first to know where he is going, to have seen the promised land and to be reasonably certain that he will better his lot by moving there with his women and children and the companions of his tribe who are of a kindred mind and spirit.

First off he will build and equip a good-sized double canoe, light but commodious and durable. On the way out it will be powered principally by paddling men, no women or other accessories, its sail rated as an auxiliary. It will be provisioned for consumption only, the most compact rations that can be prepared, calculated to support the men for a maximum number of days.

Several voyages would be contemplated running out on angled courses like the outstretched fingers on a flattened hand pointed eastward. Every "finger" would be a preselected star path carefully memorized night after night, year after year on the home island, each one marked ahead by a series of stars in the east, and astern by a series in the west. The intention would be to run out on a finger for each voyage until a suitable island or island group was found. They would paddle and sail, out to their point of no return against the prevailing easterlies and therefore against the current. Just how well these double canoes could tack against the wind is a moot question. A professor at the University of California, Dr. C. O. Bechtol, has made some carefully scientific experiments with model canoes and concludes that "all types of oceanic canoes can successfully sail to windward." One of his models based on the plans of Admiral Paris was able to sail to within about sixty degrees. When you realize that Captain Cook could probably do no better than seventy-five degrees and Magellan's galleons not nearly as well as that you realize that most of the exploration and sailing trade of the western world was accomplished with vessels less efficient to windward than the Polynesian canoe. So, often a good slant of wind would enable them to raise the sail and help them along, but mainly these preliminary exploratory voyages would be paddle-power ones until they felt they must turn around and come back under sail before the wind and with the current; all downhill, as a sailor would say.

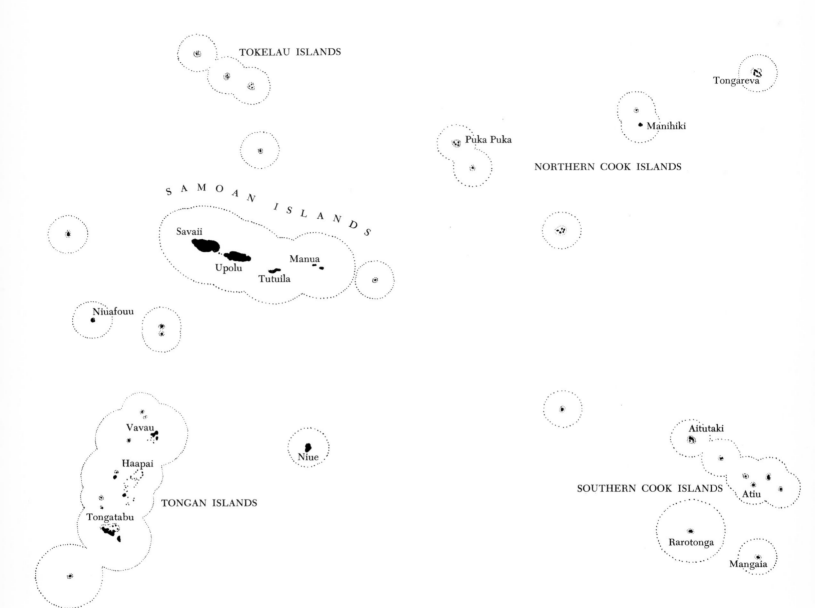

TOKELAU ISLANDS

Tongareva

Puka Puka

Manihiki

NORTHERN COOK ISLANDS

S A M O A N   I S L A N D S

Savaii

Upolu

Manua

Tutuila

Niuafouu

Vavau

Niue

Aitutaki

Haapai

SOUTHERN COOK ISLANDS

Atiu

TONGAN ISLANDS

Tongatabu

Rarotonga

Mangaia

Dr. David Lewis in 1964 was the first, as far as I know, to show graphically and convincingly how groups of islands offered "screens" as targets for the Polynesian navigator. He drew a radius of 30 miles around each island because that is generally considered a conservative estimate of the distance from which a good Polynesian seaman could, by the various offshore means at his disposal, detect the presence of land. Dr. Lewis disregarded heights which, if fairly considerable, add another 20 miles, but the high islands

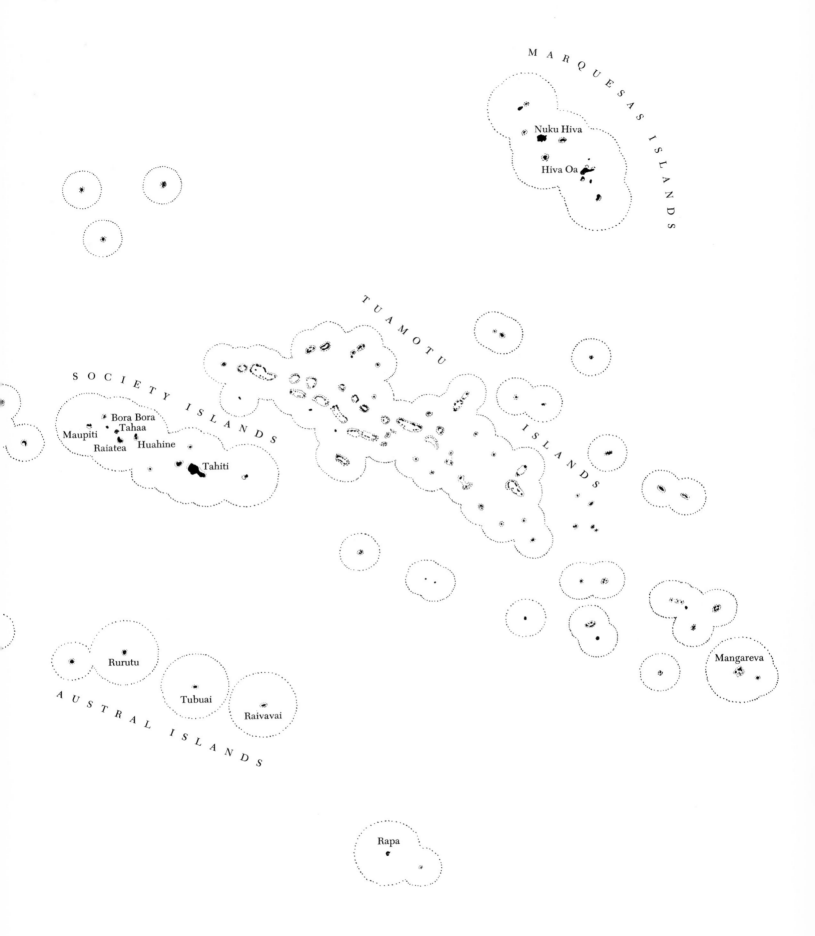

on this map have been given their 50 mile due. It can readily be seen how the islands "interlock" to give the navigator very considerable spreads for landfalls. Indeed if he could keep going far enough on an exploratory voyage on even the most approximate easterly or westerly course, he was bound to wind up in an island cluster.

J. P. Frankel considers that a radius of 60 miles can be allowed and Dr. William Van Dorn has seen Mauna Loa 90 miles at sea in the daytime.

On such a voyage they would probably figure a time ratio of about 3 to 1; let us say twenty-four days out and eight days back; thirty-two days in all. Twenty-four days at 50 miles per day gives them a range of 1200 miles. This is almost exactly the distance from Savaii to Raiatea, the longest west-east hitch in sub-equatorial Polynesia. This means a speed made good of only 2 knots which in turn means that the double canoe would have to be paddled or sailed through the water, with wind and current mostly against it, at an average of about 3 to 3½ knots each twenty-four hours for twenty-four days. Ben Finney, as one of his anthropological research projects, has recently commenced a series of carefully planned and controlled experiments to measure food consumption, oxygen and energy intake and output in an ocean-going, twin-hulled canoe that he has built in Hawaii. The results should soon tell us whether or not these estimates fall within the bounds of probability.

Mind you this is an arbitrary choice and the most arduous one that could be laid out. Even so it seems reasonable on the face of it and actually there is considerable leeway here, for Maupiti lies 50 miles west of Raiatea, and Manua is 100 miles east of Savaii. Assuming Maupiti could be seen or sensed 50 miles away (it is a high island), we have gained nearly four days, reducing the outward-bound projection to twenty days and thus the necessary average speed to more like 3 knots. Once Maupiti is sighted, it would be simple to go on to Raiatea, refresh for a few days and return downwind with a new set of star paths firmly established. These figures are a good deal more conservative than those assumed by most writers.

As soon as the paddlers had returned from a successful island-finding trip, the next step would be to organize an expedition of several canoes completely provisioned with women, pigs, dogs, chickens, roots, and shoots of a dozen plants, and a quantity of coconuts, all for colonizing the new land as well as providing rations for the voyage. Progress would be slower, so an outbound trip more like thirty days would be envisioned.

On clear nights even a certain amount of tacking against the wind could be done when they had a particularly clear star lineup. They would simply run back to their guiding star path every so often. This meant more sailing and less paddling, but by now they had the security of an established route and could substitute wind power to a sizable degree for paddle power. Tacking against the wind may have been slower, but it was a lot easier and the elimination of the uncertainty of an unknown destination and of the need to provide for a return voyage would make an enormous difference. If you know what you are in for, you can make it a lot more comfortably.

Auxiliary power is something that Columbus and Cook conceived not of and yet how wonderfully useful and how always at hand for the Polynesians who had their paddles. They had a powerful motor long before we developed ours as a significant element in navigation; moreover, it was always ready to perform, regardless of the battery charge or the cleanliness of the carburetor. Of course the old whalers sent out their boats to tow the big ship when she was in serious trouble, but the limitations are evident compared to a true auxiliary motor; the paddles in a canoe. When this is appreciated and when you realize that the early explorers could conceive of no other way to move a ship except with a favorable wind, you realize that their reports very naturally lacked a whole dimension which was of great importance. Even the modern navigational expert ignores this critical course-adjusting facility.

To include the settlement of Easter Island in this deliberate return-voyage theory would seem to stretch it very far. And yet Dr. Peter Buck (or Te Rangi Hiroa, as he was known in his native Maori tongue) felt confident that some Polynesians sailed to South America (which they could not have missed) and fetched back the sweet potato. Coming or going, conceivably they hit upon *Te Pito O Te Henua*, "The Navel of the Earth," and were able to settle it with a well-manned, well-womaned, and well-floraed canoe that had aboard, at the very least, a fertile hen and a pregnant rat. Conceivable, but barely so; more likely one lucky accident, though the myths recorded by Father Sebastian who lived on the island for nearly thirty-five years say that Hau Maka of Hiva saw the island in a dream and sent seven young men to reconnoiter it before its founding father, Hotu Matua, set out. Unfortunately for our theory Hotu Matua arrived before the seven returned. On the other hand ethnological evidence indicates that there were two distinct branches of the population, and this would mean at least two discoveries.

Most all of the believers in deliberate voyaging have assumed that the big voyages were made when the winds were most "favorable"; these are the seasonal west winds that blow during the summer months of the rainy season late in November through February and into March; out on the west wind, back on the east. Perhaps, but this is also the time of storms and of fickle weather. Canoes making short voyages between familiar islands such as we know were made between Bora Bora and Tahiti could take advantage of these favorable, seasonal winds. But they are not good months for long exploratory voyages into the unknown. All the rest of the year, six or seven months to be conservative, are to us unbelievably constant and fair. I have cruised a whole month in the Marquesas during March and April when we got no more than three or four showers and they of less than a half hour's duration, and hardly a capful of wind in them. This is normal weather in these parts, in these seasons, 2,000 miles east and west between Samoa and the Marquesas, 600 miles north and south between the latitude of Tahiti and the latitude of Nuku Hiva. Nowhere else in the world is there such reliable, smiling weather, stars ablaze at night, steady trade winds to temper the tropic sun by day. The only blemish is the scarcity of rain squalls to provide drinking water.

A factor that must always be kept in mind is current, but in this great sub-equatorial rectangle on east/west courses, it is of little hindrance to navigation because the surface currents run with the wind, the same way; either with you or against you, either slowing you down or speeding you up; in neither case taking you laterally off your course to any alarming degree. Indeed new refinements of ocean current study by Tumarkin present evidence of a south equatorial counter-current that would have been favorable to easterly voyages even when the trades were against them. On north/south voyages currents are an altogether different matter, but on east/west voyages there is nothing unpredictable about them; they become solely a consideration of time. The idea that canoes could easily lose their ways at sea on account of current during these benign months in these benign latitudes can be virtually dismissed.

The most formidable opponent of such roseate views is a retired Swedish naval officer named Kjell Akerblom, who has recently published a masterful review and summary of all the evidence that he considers permissible and arrives at the conclusion that no purposeful voyaging of over 300 miles could ever have taken place. He proves it to his own satisfaction, basing his proof on what he considers facts alone and rejecting all conjecture or hypothesis. This represents a strict scientific attitude that he and many other conservative scientists feel is the only allowable approach. Facts are not facts unless they are provable, and thus he limits himself to the sort of evidence that in our own law courts would prove or disprove a crime. Unfortunately the Polynesian committed his crime of commandeering all those islands without the kind of witnesses whom Akerblom's rules would allow him to accept, namely, the people themselves; and still more unfortunately without leaving any written record of their doings.

But Akerblom cannot be discounted just because he seems to lack consideration for human ingenuity. Contrary to Andrew Sharp, he does concede the practicability of steering by "horizon" stars. His analyses are welcome for their detail and precision especially in contrasting and comparing the techniques of the different areas of Micronesia, although his exposure of these complexities and adjustments to them seems to defeat his broad conviction that these people were of such limited and primitive mental capacities that they could not accomplish their long-distance migrations except by accident.

He is apparently aware of the possibility of a fore-and-aft star method in reciting Kramer's reports from Samoa, but in choosing to discredit Kramer and confusing a two-star concept with Reche's three-star one, he does not give it more than passing consideration. But however carefully I follow him, I cannot find that he disproves this theory, though I suspect he would reject it.

But we are embarked here on the winds and waves that have carried men to the beckoning stars. We must give professional navigators and scriptural scientists our consideration, modify our superlatives, qualify our enthusiasms, and caution our conclusions. Consider them, yes, but leave them in their neat little niches and pass them by; to accept their gospel is to negate creation and evolution. We are trying to discover the sea road of exploration leading to settlement, and if too much consideration had been given to the prophets of the impossible in the past, there never would have been any settlement at all.

Polynesian navigation was not all-inclusive as ours became at the time of Captain Cook and has been since. Theirs was not a comprehensive scientific system but rather a localized art depending on experience and observation alone, limited to their geographical living quarters and to east/west courses to and from clusters of islands in equatorial latitudes. It was perhaps a crude arrangement, but so was ours crude until fairly recent times. The maritime historian, E. G. R. Taylor, in her *The Haven-Finding Art* says that "medieval sailing [A. D. 500 to 1500] had no relation to latitude or longitude," and she adds that the compass was probably not used until the later part of this period, long after the Polynesian was comfortably settled on many of his distant islands.

Crude navigation it may have been, but it served him tolerably well. And in spite of all the contentions to the contrary, it served him as well for long distances as it did for short. The argument that drift or current would take him off his course progressively and cumulatively is an assumption based on our scientific method of locating ourselves on a latitude/longitude grid and not on his empirical method of locating himself on a star-fixed course. He might never know just where he was on this course (until he got there), but every night or at least every few nights he could correct and dispose of his drift and his current displacement by lining up his canoe on his two key stars and their precursors and successors that made up the memorized star path.

If this method worked at all, it worked as well at the end of the voyage as it did at the beginning. It worked as well for a thousand miles as it did for a hundred.

And thus we may reenvision the great west-east migrations: first a series of exploratory voyages to locate new islands suitable for settlement; voyages powered largely by paddle on the way out against the winds, undertaken in the best of weather, following set courses, guided precisely fore and aft by carefully memorized star sequences during the nights and roughly during the days by sunrise and sunset positions adjusted in accord with the seasons, ranging from one screen of islands astern to another screen of islands ahead to furnish wide margins for error. Secondly came the follow-up voyage on the newly established track, probably a fleet or group of canoes carrying the whole variegated household to found a new island colony. Altogether it seems hardly possible that the Polynesian voyagers could miss, providing they could stick with it long enough. And that leads us to the next critical considerations of staying power and of provisioning. Their vessels must be strong and durable to contend successfully with the sea. Their food and water must be ample and incorruptible to keep their crews in trim.

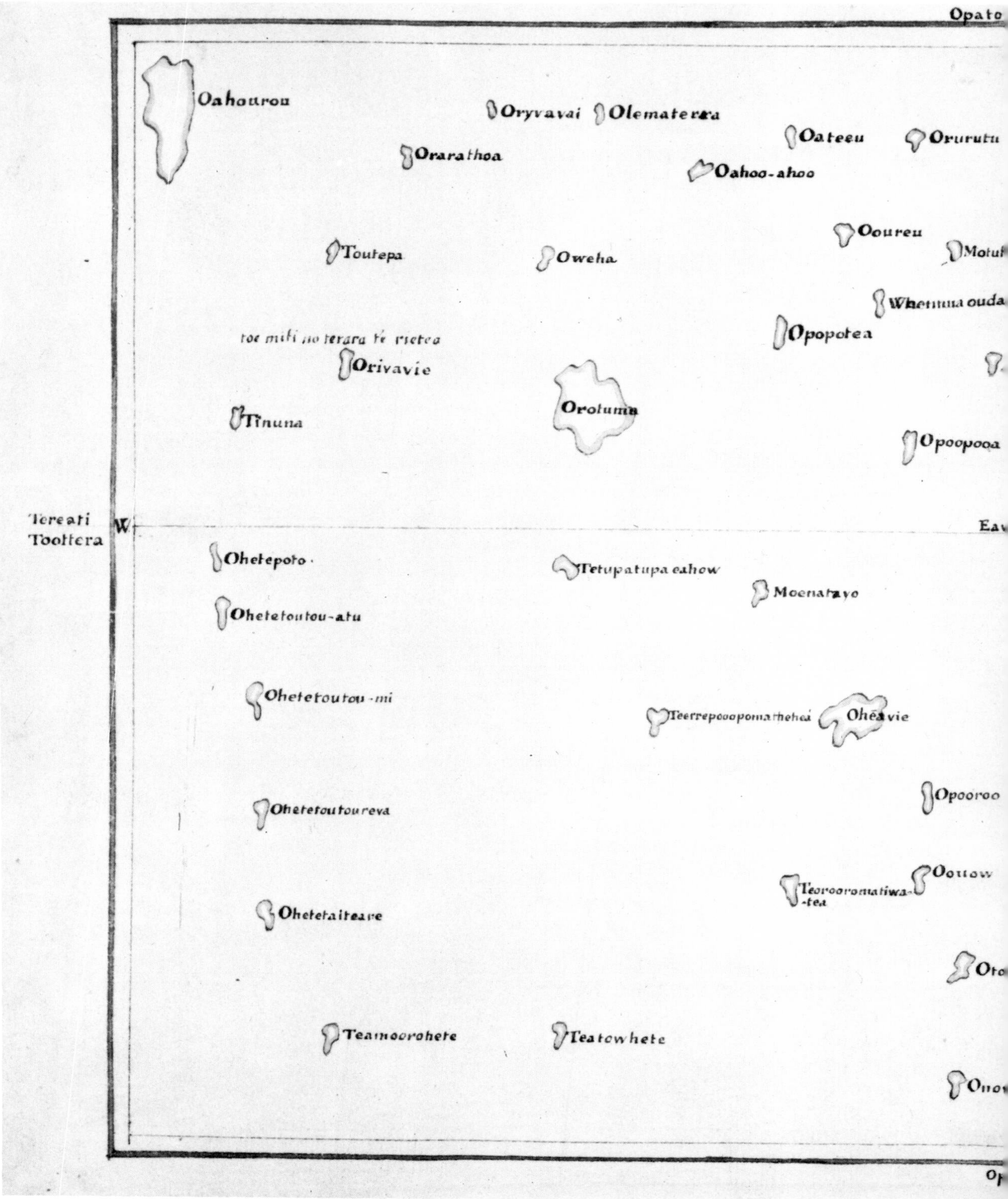

Oahourou

Oryvavai Olematerra

Orarathoa

Oateeu Orurutu

Oahoo-ahoo

Ooureu

Motu

Toutepa Oweha

Whennua ouda

Opopotea

toe mifi no terara te rietea

Orivavie

Orolunu

Tinuna

Opoopooa

Tereati W
Toottera

Eaw

Ohetepoto

Tetupatupa eahow

Moenatayo

Ohetetoutou-atu

Ohetetoutou-mi

Teerrepooopoma thehei Oheavie

Ohetetoutoureva

Opooroo

Oouow

Teorooromatiwa--tea

Ohetetaiteare

Oto

Teamoorohete Teatowhete

Ono

Tupaia was a tahuna or arii (chief) from Raiatea whom Cook picked up on his first voyage because of his extraordinary knowledge of Polynesian geography and his amazing ability to converse in the other island dialects. He sometimes directed Cook to "discoveries" of new islands and from the time he joined the Endeavor in July 1769 until they arrived in Batavia in December 1770, he was always able to point correctly to the direction of Tahiti even though they rounded the southern end of New Zealand and coasted Australia.

About midway on the voyage, Cook got Tupaia to make a "Chart of the Islands Drawn by Tupia's own hands" (no doubt with much assistance from Cook, because cartography was completely unknown in Polynesia). The original does not seem to have survived, but this is a copy of it apparently drawn by Cook. Amongst scholars it has become a highly controversial document, but our best authority on it is Professor J. C. Beaglehole, who recently completed massive annotated editions of the Journals of both Cook and Banks. Here is a somewhat abbreviated quotation of Beaglehole's comment on Tupaia's "Chart."

"This list [of the names on the chart] is not altogether hopeless as [Capt. W. J. L.] Wharton roundly declares, but as a guide to the Pacific it certainly leaves something to be desired. It is complicated not merely by the fact that Cook was reducing a strange language to writing, and running prefixes into names, but by the further facts that some

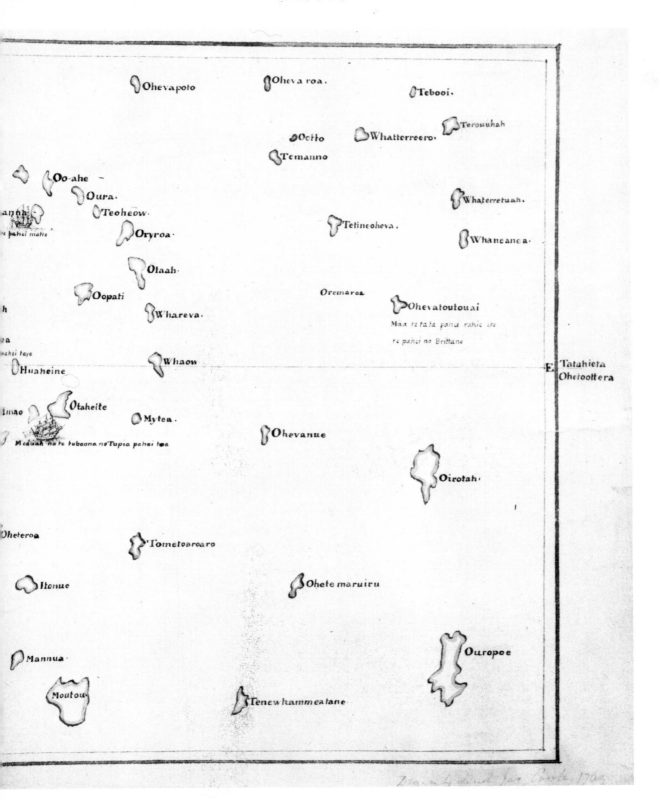

of the names are evidently ancient ones not now used, and that the directions in which they lie are sometimes considerably out—either because of erroneous information from Tupaia or because his information was misunderstood. At the same time one must remember that quite different islands often had identical names. It is possible to identify, either certainly, or to the point of near certainty, between forty and fifty, and close study by a deep Polynesian scholar would probably make fairly good sense of the whole list [73]; but a few examples may be brought forward to illustrate what has been said. In the 'NE Quarter' we may recognize some of the Tuamotu atolls: e.g. Oopate=Apata[k]i; Oryroa=Rairoa; Whareva=Fa[k]arava. In the same quarter Ohevaroa is evidently Hivaoa in the Marquesas, and Ohevapato, similarly, Fatu Hiva. In the 'NW Quarter' Opopatea is Papatea, an old name for Makatea; Oahooahoo is Ahuahu, the old name for Mangaia. In the 'S.W. Quarter' have been incorrectly put the Samoan islands of Tutuila or Otootooera, and Upolu or Opooroo; but, correctly, Haapai in Tonga—if that is the particular Hawaii or Hawai'i meant by Oheavie. The atoll Fenua Ura (Whennuaouda) may be said to be in the right direction, however, and no doubt this would prove to be true of many others. In Moutou we have an old name, evidently for Tubuai, due S of Tahiti. 'Pooromathehea' is an extraordinary problem, though not the only one: taking a long shot, I risk the suggestion that Cook has misread his rough notes."

CONSTRUCTION AND DESIGN
Many Canoes of Many Kinds

Seafaring is, of course, journeying by sea, and the Polynesian made many sorts of journeys in his watery world. For each of them he devised a special craft suitable to its special purpose. Most people realize that his canoes were many and that he was clever with them, but few are aware of the considerable variety and specializations that he developed; so diverse that it is superficial of us to call them all canoes and to think of them merely as dugouts with shapes fluctuating on account of whims, or styles, or different island conditions. Actually they were most ingeniously designed and constructed to serve their several different purposes so that taken as a whole they comprise a maritime body more varied and particularized than that of any other nonindustrial culture, simply because the Polynesians were seafaring to a degree to which no other culture had ever adapted.

*   *   *

"Dr. Solander and myself walkd out this morn and saw many large boat-houses like that describd at Huahine page 303 and 401. On these the inhabitants were at work makeing and repairing the large Canoes called by them Pahee,* at which business they workd with incredible cleverness tho their tools were certainly as bad as possible. I will first give the dimensions and description of one of their boats and then their method of building. Its extreme length from stem to stern not reckoning the bending up of both those parts 51 feet; breadth in the clear at the top forward 14 inches, midships 18, aft 15; in the bilge forward 32 inches, midships 35, aft 33; depth midships 3 ft 4; hight from the ground she stood on 3 ft 6; her head raisd without the figure 4 ft 4 from the ground, the figure 11 inches; her stern 8 ft 9, the figure 2 feet. Alongside of her was lashd another like her in all parts but less in proportion being only 33 feet in her extreme lengh. The form of these Canoes is better to be expressed by a drawing than by any description. This

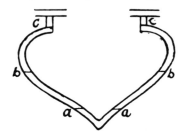

annexd may serve to give some Idea of a section: *aa* is the first seam, *bb* the second, *cc* the third. The first stage or keel under *aa* is made of trees hollowd out

---

*pahi. The people of Raiatea were the great canoe-builders of the Society group. The description which Banks proceeds to give us is more detailed than anything in Cook.

like a trough for which purpose they chuse the longest trees they can get,* so that 2 or three make the bottom of their largest boats (some of which are much larger than that described here as I make a rule to describe every thing of this kind from the common size); the next stage under *bb* is formd of streght plank about 4 feet long and 15 inches broad and 2 inches thick; the next stage under *cc* is made like the bottom of trunks of trees hollowd into its bilging form; the last or that above *cc* is formd also out of trunks of trees so that the moulding is of one peice with the plank. This work difficult as it would be to an Europaean with his Iron tools they perform without Iron and with amazing dexterity; they hollow with their stone axes as fast at least as our Carpenters could do and dubb tho slowly with prodigious nicety; I have seen them take off a skin of an angular plank without missing a stroke, the skin itself scarce 1/16 part of an inch in thickness. Boring the holes throug[h] which their sewing is to pass seems to be their greatest difficulty. Their tools are made of the bones of men, generaly the thin bone of the upper arm; these they grind very sharp and fix to a handle of wood, making the instrument serve the purpose of a gouge by striking it with a mallet made of of a hard black wood,† and with them would do as much work as with Iron tools was it not that the brittle Edge of the tool is very liable to be broke.

"When they have prepard their planks &c. the keel is layd on blocks and the whole Canoe put together much in the same manner as we do a ship, the sides being supported by stantions and all the seams wedg'd together before the last sewing is put on, so that they become tolerably tight considering that they are without calking.‡

"With these boats they venture themselves out of sight of land; we saw several of them at Otahite which had come from Ulhietea and Tupia has told us that they go voyages of twenty days, whether true or false I do not affirm. They keep them very carefully under such boathouses as are described p. 316, one of which we measured today 60 yards by 11."—*Sir Joseph Banks, 1769 (footnotes by J. C. Beaglehole, 1962)*

*   *   *

The word *canoe* comes from the Carib, *canaoa*, so it was probably brought back to Europe by Columbus, and every craft seen thereafter in the western hemisphere and later by association, in Indonesia, Indochina, and the Pacific became a "canoe," whether of birch bark, walrus hide, or wood; whether 10 feet long or a hundred; whether double, single, or outrigger; whether sailed or paddled.

It is commonly stated that "canoes" derived originally from floating logs, and hence outriggers or doubling up were invented to keep them from rolling over. This is one of those deductive absurdities that used to come so easily to early students of mankind; the old and, alas, still present conceit that our early ancestors were "primitive," that is, incapable of matching our own brilliant feats of intellect.

---

*The timbers used for canoe-building were mainly Faifai *(Serianthes myriadenia)*, a large valley-growing tree, a favorite for *pahi;* the Uru or breadfruit, and the Hutu *(Barringtonia speciosa)*.

†Toa or ironwood.

‡This is evidently a mistake. Caulking was done with fine coconut fiber and the adhesive sap of the breadfruit used as pitch; but Banks probably did not see the process.

A canoe no more evolved from a nonrolling log than the wheel from a rolling stone. A canoe was a hollow structure, a "vessel," floating high on the water, conceived and built to carry a burden with ease and speed. The wheel is often considered the greatest break-through invention of mankind, respected even today and compared with such technological miracles as the combustion engine and the splitting of the atom. Its invention is presumed to have taken place between six and ten thousand years ago.

Well, the canoe or the ship,* as we have called our European equivalent, may not, perhaps, be ranked with the wheel, but even so it might be recognized as a momentous technological event, probably of equal and perhaps of even more distant antiquity. The wheel was the landsman's wonder; the canoe was the waterman's. They both got him up on the surface and sped him, not effortlessly, but wonderously well on his wandering way.

For the Polynesian this was not just one technological creation but a whole series of them. Naturally there was a good deal of overlapping, but the main categories are quite distinct.

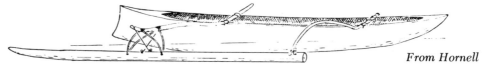

From Hornell

1. The small paddling outrigger canoe, 10-20 feet long, used mostly for fishing within the reef or not far offshore, the *vaa*. Neat vessels they were and are, delicately shaped and balanced with outriggers pegged and seized in many ingenious ways, each one with its own particular and characteristic style, indeed ritualistic, so that they declare each island's individuality even among such closely gathered groups as the "Societies." Hornell distinguishes unmistakably by its outrigger attachment a Huahine canoe from a Moorea one.

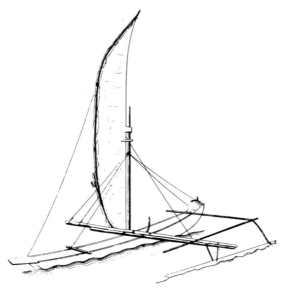

From Paris

*In the Indo-European languages there are many variations of the word *ship* (or vessel), all obviously related, but the root of the word is unknown. It is interesting that *Ship* and *Vehicle* are co-listed in Roget's *Thesaurus*.

2. The smaller sailing outrigger canoe, 20-30 feet as a rule, but sometimes larger, used for deep-sea fishing primarily, but also for short inter-island voyaging, usually equipped with a balancing platform, the *vaa ta'ie*. Beautiful vessels these were, works of sea-going art, for they were all-utility, marvelously efficient with the minimum of material.

This Micronesian canoe by Choris illustrates the one-sided curve of the hull that pre-vented or, at least, offset leeway.

3. The larger sailing outrigger canoe, 30-50 feet, most of them Micronesian, used for long-range deep-sea sailing between island groups. And these as refined sailing machines were the best of all. They had not the stability, strength, and capability to contend with all sorts of deep-sea, long-slugging operations that were the challenge of the great ocean-going double canoes, but for somewhat shorter, though not inconsiderable, distances in fair weather and more certain objectives, they were the most efficient sailing machines ever designed. It will not be long before we recognize that our *America*'s Cup contenders are clumsy in comparison.

From Ellis

69

From Ellis

4. The small double canoe, 20-40 feet, with flat prows and upturned sterns used for voyaging within the reef to carry passengers and cargo, and for the shorter inter-island voyages; often bearing a small house between hulls for shade, sleep, eating, etc., and a sandbox forward for a cooking fire. When rigged with a special long pole, they were used for bonita and other open-ocean fishing. This *tahifa*, or all-around work vessel, was sometimes rigged with one mast, more often with two, and carried lateen sails, the *vaa hara*. Its upturned sterns warded off the waves when it was beached and its flat, protruding bows provided gang planks to walk, laden, ashore. They make our present-day intra-lagoon carriers seem tipsy and inefficient.

* * *

"Their was Several Large double Canoes came off with her this Morning which came from the S.W. end of the Bay last night, in Each of this canoes, their was a very Convenient place where ten or a dozen people could sit under a canopy, it was built not unlyke the place where Gentlemen Sits in the City Barges, altho not so finely decorated, in this Large Canoes their was a great Many familys of Jolly fatt well made people, and mutch fairer nor any that we ever saw before, the two Young Ladys which the Queen introduced me to only Excepted, they were likeways drest mutch netaer, nor any of the people which we saw before, all the Servents which paddled this great Canoes was of a coper colour and their masters and mistresses seemd to have a great power over them, the whole of the fair people sit under the Canopys."—*George Robertson, 1767*

* * *

5. The large single-hull war canoes of the New Zealand Maori, running up to 100 feet. These were the only single-hulled, that is, non-outrigger or non-double canoes, in Polynesia. Since they were a late development whose beam was made possible only because of the hugeness of New Zealand forest trees, and since they were used for coastal warfare only, they will be virtually disregarded in this book. Magnificent structures though they were, they cannot be classed as ocean-going vessels. They seemed to have been designed more for show and prestige than for military utility. They were more works of art than use, their bow and stern carvings being perhaps the ultimate aesthetic expression of Maori sculpture.

70

From Hawkesworth

From Cook's Atlas

6. The large double war canoes (Cook measured one of 108 feet) propelled by paddlers only, upturned bows and highly upturned sterns, with a raised platform for warriors and chiefs. Occurring chiefly in Tahiti, these were the largest vessels built in eastern Polynesia, being excelled in size only by the huge Tongan *tongiaki*. They were called *pahi tamai* and, like the Maori war canoes, were not true seafarers although they did voyage over more than a hundred miles of open sea between Raiatea and Tahiti. In them the upswinging stems were protection from oncoming missiles and the soaring sterns not only shielded their rear but gave them a fighting altitude.

7. The large double voyaging canoes for exploration and distant ocean transport. We know very little of these because they were extinct or virtually so when the first European came to the Pacific. The large Hawaiian double canoes were probably the nearest relatives we know at all well, but by the time of Cook these were interisland rather than ocean going. They were paddled as well as sailed and probably were not highly upturned in bows or sterns, the *pahi tere*.

71

Though the recorded evidence of the particulars is scantier than any of the other types of canoe, it is with this last class that this book is chiefly concerned. We may not know very well exactly what they looked like, but we do know how they performed, and this performance is almost certainly the most remarkable of any naturally propelled maritime vessel ever developed.

Pirogue double, des Isles Sandwich,
Fig. 2, Page 484.

From Lescallier

Introduction to the Groups of Pictures

The groups of pictures that follow at intervals hereafter make this section on construction and design largely pictorial. They have been arranged in more or less chronological order within the geographical groups of islands. Such a scheme, or any other scheme, is subject to the whims of the material available, that is, what the artists or other recorders chose to draw and what they chanced to see. Unfortunately no one, except Admiral Paris somewhat late in the day, was assigned the job of surveying and recording the watercraft of Polynesia. Some captains and some artists took an interest in maritime artifacts, others were more concerned with humanity, botany, scenery, so the results are haphazard, but fortunately there is enough to show how numerous and prevalent canoes were throughout Polynesia. The illustrations here were sought and selected preferably for prime source material, that is, field sketches, drawings, and paintings by the artists rather than the published renditions by the engravers back home. Indeed in some cases, especially those from the Cook voyages, the engravings are omitted because they are so easily available in other books to anyone interested. The usual procedure, of course, was to make rough sketches and measurements on the spot, to fashion a more finished drawing or wash painting on board ship and then to do an oil painting or more elaborated renditions back home in London or Paris. Also the artist presumably aided the steel engraver, although the engravers often made errors and omissions, and details no doubt often slipped the memory of the artist on the long voyage home. Most of these sketches have been published only in specialized journals or books; some have not been published at all and I have not seen before comparisons that illustrated the various steps.

The pictures have been gathered in geographical groups because, although a Polynesian canoe is unmistakable no matter where it comes from, each island cluster had its own style and comparing the vessels within it and the styles of the different artists brings out more of the subtleties of shaping, rigging, construction, etc., than would be apparent if, say, they were grouped according to size or function from all the segments of the ocean.

This book is concerned primarily with long-range voyaging and therefore with the double canoe, so that practically every recording of this type of vessel will be seen even if some of them, such as illustrate the missionaries' books, are obviously not in all ways accurate. But in some cases, the most important being the Marquesas, there are no recordings of double canoes even though we know they existed. However, since the double canoe was frequently made up of the hulls of two single (outrigger) canoes, pictures are shown of single hulls to show the local types and in some instances to illustrate details that probably were common to both.

The sources are as many and as widely chosen as possible. Everyone is familiar with the marvelous work both in quantity and in quality of Cook's artists, Sydney Parkinson, William Hodges, and James Webber. They alone might suffice to illustrate the subject. But it is interesting and sometimes revealing to compare how others saw and drew the same craft.

Tonga *comes first because it was the first to be recorded. The* Society *group has the largest collection. War canoes are presented separately because although they were not long-distance, deep-sea vessels, yet their great size and intricate construction are a valuable attestation of the shipbuilder's art. Recordings of double canoes from the* Other Island Groups *are so scarce that they are all placed together in the next section. Models are numerous in museums, but early, authentic ones are rare so these, except for the unusually interesting Manihiki type that is recorded only in models, serve as a sort of review. The* Single Hull *outriggers were not used for long-distance voyaging except in Micronesia, but they show interesting nautical details and give us the widest range of artists. The* Plans *are mostly the meticulous work of F. E. Paris who went along with Dumont D'Urville.*

Tongan Canoes

The double canoes of Tonga were, as far as we know, the largest of any built in Polynesia. Because the central ocean islands were so much more distant, there may have been others to equal them in the Societies or Marquesas, but there was no evidence of any such when the Europeans arrived. But great size is no perquisite of ability to travel great distance and therefore no basis for competitive comparison. The Tongan voyages of historical or believably semi-historical record were relatively short, not more than 500 miles at the most. But their vessels were huge and their seamanship astonishing. G. S. Parsonson recapitulates them well in Polynesian Navigation. *They and the closely related Fijian vessels sometimes measured as much as 100 feet and were capable of carrying a couple of hundred persons.*

On the following page are probably the first pictorial recordings of double canoes. They were seen by Schouten in 1616 in the northern part of the Tongan group.

The second view close to land shows four of these tongiaki *and perhaps an attack on the Dutch vessel which may, at least in their minds, have justified the pursuit and shooting above. Forster who came to the Tongan Islands with Cook later on in 1777 says that a "rude figure of a tortoise or a cock is sometimes represented" on their sails. Cocos was later called Boscoween and is Niutoputapu. Verrardors was Traitors Island, later Keppel, and is Tafahi.*

Cocos Eylandt

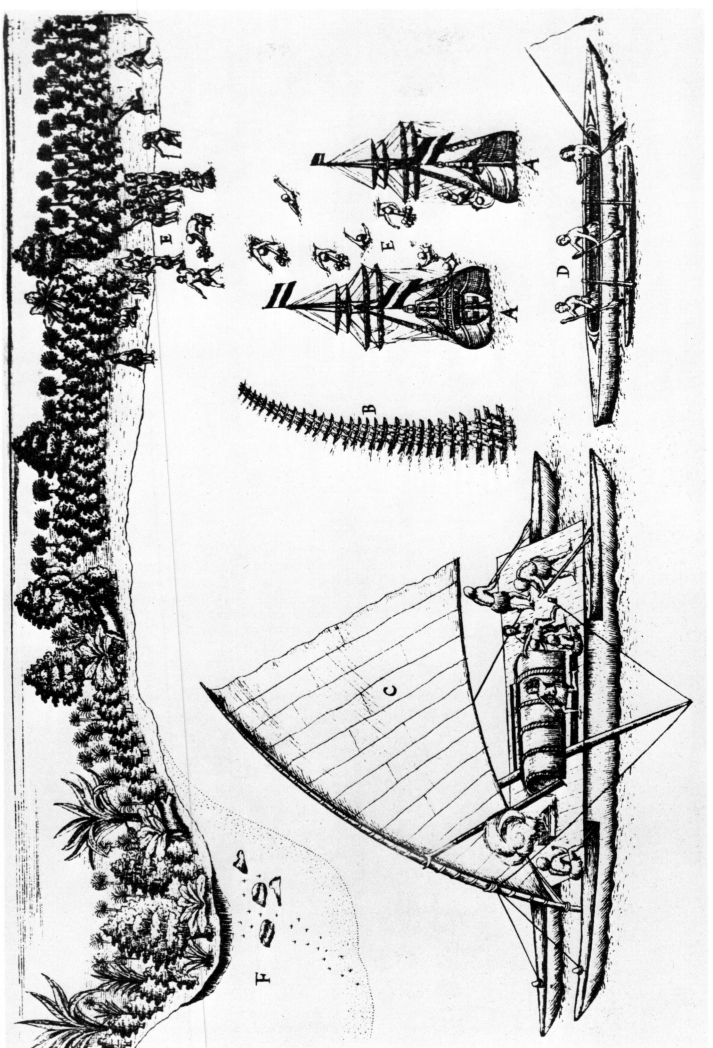

This is a more accurate and detailed drawing of a Tongan tongiaki by Tasman in 1642.

Another view shows two of these double canoes, moored and dismasted.

Although Mendana and Quiros in 1595 and Le Maire and Schouten in 1616 undoubtedly were the first Europeans to see Polynesian double canoes, the best early written report comes from Abel Tasman, 1642, from Tonga.

"The next day a strange canoe ran before the bow of the flute Zee-haen. Two sloops, fastened together, and with bamboos laid over the sides, bore several men, directed by a chief who told some to be silent, others to sit, others to run below or to row. All obeyed. In the middle of the deck of the two craft stood a hut, plaited arch-like out of bamboos and covered with banana-leaves. The Sail was of mats and made a smart progress."

This picture is a rather amusing example of illustrative plagiarism. It is obviously the same drawing slightly modified, the frontispiece of an unauthorized account written anonymously well over a hundred years later in 1775 by one of the members of Cook's crew.

Hodges, who was Cook's artist on his second voyage, almost certainly made this wash →
drawing on the spot. Later on, probably when he was back in England, he executed this
large oil painting. It is apparently an adaptation and elaboration of the field sketch. Note
the turtle this time instead of the cock on the sail.

Webber, Cook's artist on his third voyage, records in this detail from a much larger wash drawing his version of a double canoe, Tongan style. It is interesting for the particulars it shows of the set and shape of the sail.

Somewhat later, 1791, Labillardiere on his voyage in search of the shipwrecked La Perouse presents his version, easily recognizable as a genuine tongiaki, nautically inaccurate but amusingly romanticized, perhaps by the Parisian engraver for the French public.

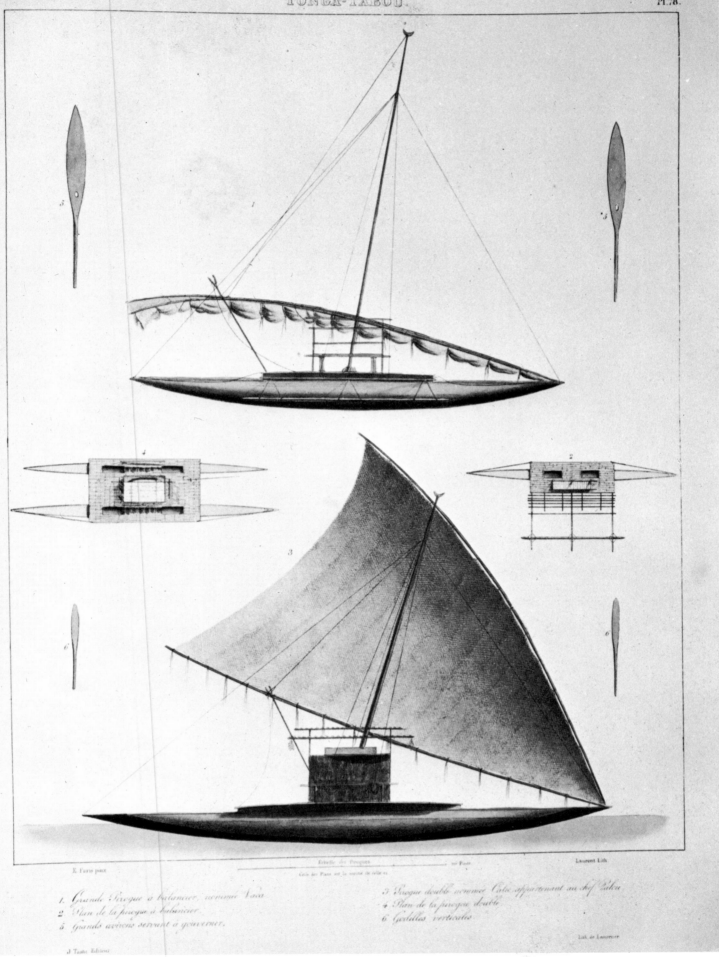

E. Paris pinx. Laurent lith.

1. *Grande Pirogue à balancier, nommée Vaca*
2. *Plan de la pirogue à balancier.*
3. *Grande aviron servant à gouverner.*
3. *Pirogue double nommée Calie appartenant au chef Palou*
4. *Plan de la pirogue double*
6. *Godilles verticales*

Still later, c. 1828, another French explorer, Dumont D'Urville, recorded in his elabo-
rate published volumes what is evidently a genuine Tongan vessel.

This wash drawing by one of D'Urville's artists is labeled "Double canoe of the Missionaries."

Dessiné par L. Le Breton Lith.ᵉ par P. Blanchard   Gide Éditeur   Lith. de Thierry Frères, à Paris

PIROGUE DOUBLE SOUS SON HANGARD

This picture, also from Dumont D'Urville, gives in its "hangard" a more intimate idea of the size of those vessels.

One outstanding consideration that should be emphasizèd, because it is a dramatic reflection of the importance of all of these canoes, is their prodigious numbers. Everywhere, even on the small islands, early European voyagers were astonished at the fleets of canoes, great and small, that put out from almost every shore to investigate the large, strange vessels from the other world, the lands beyond Hawaiki, the great single-hulled *pahi* in which the *papalangi*, or sky-breakers, had pierced the outer heavens to reach the islands of *Moana*.

*   *   *

"At sun rise about three hundred canoes came off and lay round the ship, as many as could conveniently lay allongside traded very fair and took nails and Toys for their Hogs, fowls and fruit, by Eight oclock their was upwards of five hundred canoes round the ship, and at a Moderate Computation there was near four thousand men—the most trading canoes which lay round the ship, and dealt with our people, had a fair young Girl in Each Canoe, who playd a great many droll wanton tricks, which drew all our people upon the Gunwells to see them, when they seemd to be most merry and friendly some of our people observd great numbers of stones in every canoe, this created a little suspition in several of our people, but the most of us could not think they hade any Bade Intention against us, Espetially as the whole traded very fair and honest, and all the men seemd as hearty and merry as the Girls.

"At this time the whole Bay was all lined round with men and women and children, to see the Onset which was now near at hand, but they still be-haved frinedly untill a large double canoe came off from the shore, with several of the Principle Inhabitance in her. This canoe lay some time on the Larbort side but keept a good distance from all the rest, and was observed to hoist some signal by some of our men, the very instant that his signall was made all trade broke up, and in a few secants of time all our Decks was full of Great and small stones, and several of our men cut and Bruisd this was so sudden and unexpected by the most of us, that we was some time before we could find out the caus, therefor orderd the sentrys to fire amongst them, in hopes that would frighten them, but this hade not the desired Effect, they all gave another shout and powerd in the stones lyke hail amongst us which hurt a great many of our men, we then found lenity would not do, therefor applyed to the Great Guns and gave them a few round and Grape shot, which struck such terror amongs the poor unhapy croad that it would require the pen of Milton to describe, therefor too mutch for mine."—*George Robertson, 1769*

*   *   *

At "Oparre," Cook "observed a number of large Canoes in Motion; but we were surprized when we got there to see upwards of three-hundred of them all rainged in good order for some distance along the Shore all Completely equip'd and Man'd." A bit further on he notes that in this fleet "the Vessels of War consisted of 160 large double Canoes." Some years later at Hawaii during his third voyage he estimates 1000 canoes about his two ships.

When you think or try to think of the man-hours that went into the building of all these craft, of the forethought, skill, ceremony, stubborn endless work, the choice of strokes, the eternal sharpening of the adzes that had themselves taken an eternity to prise and chip and grind, the considerations of soaking rain or burning sun or drying wind, the choice between another hour or two of adzing or

81

another or two of fishing or feasting, the disappointment of seeing a large flaw grow larger and of deciding that a half-finished hull dragged down from the mountainside must be abandoned, or suffer the frustration of a malevolent swipe by an enemy in the night . . .

But then you must think of the time they had and how they might have used it. There was no hastening always on to make more and more dollars. There was only the passing of a lifetime in the island sun; no notion of progress; only of making the best you can within the time you have. And your time, of course, was only part of your grandfather's and your grandson's time. These canoes took months to fashion; months of care, patience, anxiety, thrill, and despair. They were unquestionably the supreme physical output of this whole society; the chief demands on its skills, its needs, its imagination, its dedication, its highest hopes.

There were exceptions. On Easter Island wood was too scarce and isolation too vast; all their characteristically Polynesian energies and powers went into the great stone statues. On the Hawaiian Islands and in New Zealand land was plentiful and productive enough to relieve the need to go far to sea. But in the main island groups of Polynesia a man lived on the water. He lived intensely on the lagoon (as he still does) as if it were a watery backyard or a clam-crab-octopus-fish garden. On a range extending 10 or 20 miles offshore, he lived more widely, a day's journey out and back gleaning large fish, porpoise, and turtles. Almost half his life was spent in canoes, as almost half of ours is spent in automobiles. To calculate his population as so many per square mile is a view we continentals should ironically realize is insular. He lived on and off of treble the acreage of his islands. And the vehicle of his wider life was his canoe.

In light of such a prevalence of time upon the surface of the sea and such a constant intimacy with it, we must again recall the absurdity of the arguments of the accidentalists; that these people were constantly permitting themselves to be blown off like the prodigal spores of a mushroom to find by chance whatever one-in-a-thousand niche they might happen upon.

Some of their canoes are rather peculiar-looking vessels unlike any built anywhere else. But there may be good reasons for these peculiarities, attributable, as most peculiarities are, to a sensible symbiosis with the peculiar island conditions. They were adapting themselves to, or perhaps taking advantage of, the rigors (and opportunities) of a unique environment. Islands have a way of making queer impositions on their inhabitants. One can find intriguing parallels and contradictions, as Sherwin Carlquist has done, between ocean island environments all over the world in terms of plants, birds, insects, snails, and, to a usually restricted degree, animals. His separateness and individuality of island life has many exciting relations and interrelations and lack of relations. But as a botanist or biologist thinking in Jurassic, sometimes in Triassic terms, he naturally pays little mind to man.

But the islands were islands to men as well. Man's time in them may have been much shorter, but his adaptations may have been much swifter and thus comparably significant. Our concern here in Polynesia, this most islandish of all island environments, is canoes. And canoes are a manifestation of man in his most imaginative adaptation to environment. Now some of us may think this beautiful and others may think it trivial, but the canoe to the Polynesian was as the airship or spaceship is becoming to us; a refined, perhaps an overly refined, exploitation of the world around about him. He had no easily perceptible need to go to those other islands so far away over the sea. But he went. He went perhaps as we are going to the moon, and he had to build marvelous craft and devise marvelous navigational techniques before he could do it. Well, whether he had to or not, he did. And we are here in this book to admire him, or, at the very least, to make an intelligent appreciation of his efforts.

COMPARATIVE INFORMATION ON SOME FAMOUS OCEAN-GOING SHIPS

CAPTAIN OR NATIONALITY	SHIP	YEARS BEFORE PRESENT	LENGTH	TONNAGE*	PASSENGERS AND CREW
Polynesian	Double canoe	±2750	60-70 ft.	40?	50-60
Viking	Gokstad open boat	±900	76½ ft.	20+	±80
Columbus	*Santa Maria*	480	80 ft.	100	39
Magellan	*Vittoria*	453	?	85	30-40
Drake	*Golden Hind*	395	75 ft.	100	60+
British	*Mayflower*	352	90 ft.	180	149
Cook	*Endeavour*	204	106 ft.	368	±85

*"Tonnage" was an arbitrary and untrustworthy measurement: unfortunately it is still the most common dimension used in England and widely on the continent. In the cases listed above, it denoted the number of "tuns" or casks of wine a vessel could carry and these casks varied in different countries. The Greeks measured by *amphorae*, many of which are still being fetched up from the bottom of ancient Mediterranean harbors. The only sort of "tonnage" that would be meaningfully comparable would be water displacement tonnages, and the calculating of them from the hazy dimensions of these vessels is far beyond the mathematical capacities of this compiler.

Society Island Canoes

The double canoes of Raiatea, Tahiti, Tahaa, and the other Society Islands are better recorded than those of any other group, probably because there were more of them and because the European visitors stayed longer in those friendly, fertile islands.

The original wash drawings on these first five pages are by Sydney Parkinson, who was Cook's artist on his first voyage, 1768-1771. They make a charming representation of life on the lagoon and of how busy and populous it must have been. These vessels are considerably smaller than the great ocean-going double canoes, but in all their variety they must reflect many of the same characteristics. Taken from the originals in the British Museum, some of these have not been published before and never have they been shown together for comparison. It will be seen that only two are alike* even though, counting the background canoes, there are at least a dozen vessels carefully depicted, nine double canoes, one sailing outrigger, two little paddlers, and even a raft. Of them only one has upturned bows and it will also be noted that this is the sole canoe (except perhaps the sterns in the canoe shed) that carries tikis. Probably it belonged to a chief or to a "priest." There are considerable though subtle variations in the sterns. Only the sails seem to be uniform.

*The ones at the tops of pages 84 and 88 seem to be the same canoe in different settings.

Double Canoes

Canoe of Ulietea

Otaheite

View at the Back of Point Venus towards Ithos the House

H. D. Spöring, another artist on Cook's first voyage, specialized in recording natural history, fish, plants, etc., but evidently he took time off one day to sketch Queen Purea's canoe. Its overlarge deckhouse seems to have been intended primarily for the comfort of its owner and her "court" when making royal visits to her shores.

A scene in Huahine from the missionary, Rev. Daniel Tyerman, who labored in the south seas for the London Missionary Society from 1821 to 1829.

William Hodges was the artist on Cook's second voyage, 1772-1775. This harbor scene is a large oil painting at the National Maritime Museum in Greenwich, undoubtedly executed after the ship returned to London. It shows many interesting details of smaller Tahitian craft in the foreground. Note the permanent backstays on the tahifa to the right. These arrived in the western yachting world only a few decades ago. The little paddle canoe in the center shows interesting outrigger attachments. Between these two is what William Ellis calls a "screened canoe," probably double. At the left, note the guying of the typical Society Island sail.

Below: This detailed stern view shows well the construction of the typical tahifa or utility double canoe used mostly in lagoons or for short inter-island voyages. Idols or tikis mounted high on carved staves were common on war canoes, so this particular vessel may have belonged to a chief. Other more common variants of this same craft can be seen in the detail from a field sketch on page 92.

Hodges

Henry Roberts

Henry Roberts

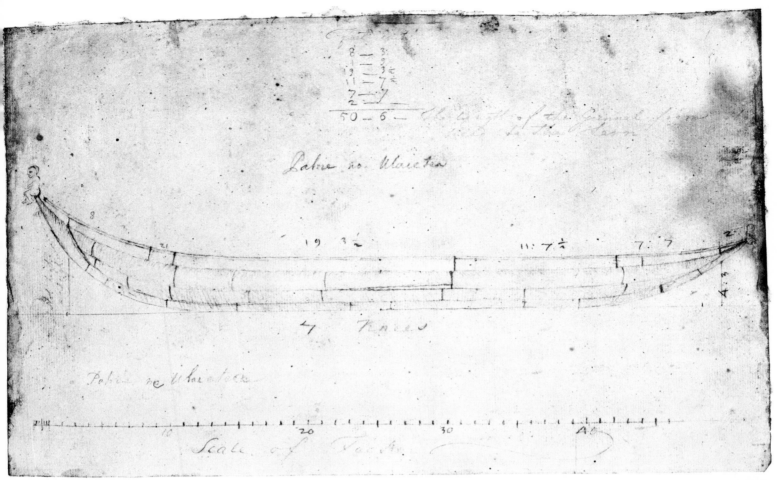

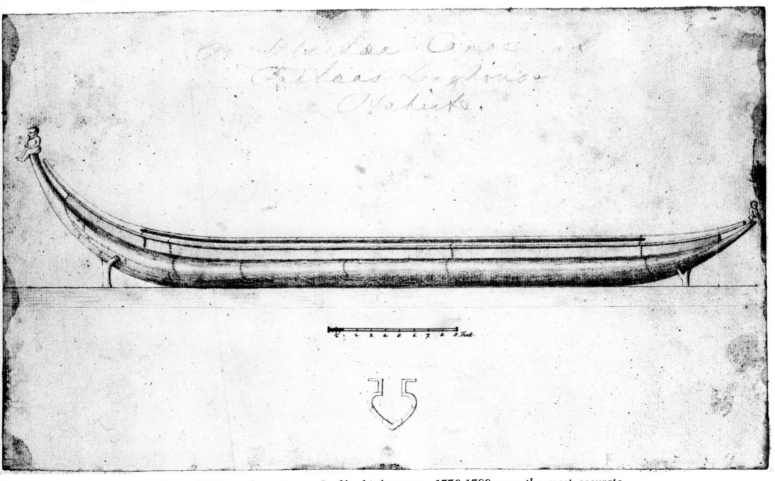

James Webber, the artist on Cook's third voyage, 1776-1780, was the most accurate observer of canoe details and construction of any of Cook's artists, but unfortunately he recorded only the one double canoe that appears on the following two pages. Here, as an introduction to his work, are two renderings of what is almost surely the same hull, a beauty, and probably, because of its size, some 50 feet, one in the process of construction for a double canoe. These sketches show how he made rough notes in the field and then refined and made some alterations when he was at his drawing board on the ship.

*Fortunately Webber's one rendering of a double canoe is a fine one. Hornell declares
it the best of any representation of a large ocean-going canoe in Polynesia. There is no
scale to show its size, but if we take the peak of the roof of the deckhouse to be 6 feet*

high (these "houses" were made low both for sitting or lying and for seaworthiness), this canoe is 96 feet overall and the hulls are 60 feet, a sizable vessel indeed. Note the typical ladder for mounting the mast.

Here is another example of a field sketch and finished drawing by Webber. It was evidently a favorite of his because it was later further refined in an aquatint and also engraved. It is most interesting for its detail and hull construction. It is not, of course, a double canoe, but it is so unusually beamy that it might be classed as a maverick. There are two double canoes in the revised background that might qualify it for this section. His depiction of the outrigger violates all the rules and customs. One can only hope that the great Webber was so interested in the uncommon hull that he was absent-minded about it.

And here for a change are some examples of inaccurate reporting. James Cleveley was the carpenter on Cook's ship and you would think he would know his small boats well enough to make careful records. Perhaps he did, but when he got back to London, they were handed over to John Cleveley, his brother, who was an artist and who turned them into three rare but widely known aquatints. Things may have been further scrambled by the publisher, Thos Martyn, for this one is labeled "Charlotte Sound," which is in New Zealand, and yet the scene (with coconut trees that do not grow there) is obviously Matavai Bay in Tahiti. Furthermore, the vessel with its sail up is unquestionably Tongan and the beached outrigger bears little or no resemblance to anything Polynesian.

The detail at the left from Cleveley's Huahine aquatint is a more accurate rendition of a tahifa, though the hulls are mistakenly lashed tight together. The other detail from Captain Wilson of the Duff, 1797, is, like all of Wilson's work, more accurate and it shows how convenient those flat bows must have been when coming ashore.

This original wash drawing of a sacred canoe of Tahiti, a sort of floating temple, is attributed by its owner, the Mitchell Library in Sydney, to William Bligh of Bounty fame. This type of vessel is another example of the maritime versatility and specialization that is so typical of the Society Island group of ancient Polynesia.

On the sketch in handwriting that is not always easily decipherable the different parts of the canoe are identified: "A—The Ephare Tuah or House of God; B—A shed placed occasionally by the side of it; C—The Morai Tebbootabooataiah; D—A kind of trough called Erroee; E—The aoy or supporters of the Epharre Etuah & Morai; F—The offering of Hogs, Fowls & a Dogs Head; G—The Eatuah Oro; H—Two Drums."

Lieutenant George Tobin was an officer on Bligh's ship who made a number of sketches and paintings of native craft with a seaman's eye for accuracy and detail. This sacred canoe seems not to be the same one recorded by his captain.

His double canoe is a somewhat vague but dashing impression of the commanding vessel of the lagoon.

We know little or nothing at all about how these canoes came to be designed except that they must gradually have acquired their virtues over long periods of time by trial and error spurred by imagination. Where and when the concept of the double canoe originated is probably a fruitless speculation. That it came from two logs seems, as has been stated, absurd, and yet it was probably the invention of what we now call straddle stability. The homeland of the outrigger canoe, both double and single, is unquestionably Indonesia or to some extent Indochina, for it occurs nowhere else in the world, except by derivation, from that generally island area. The double canoe most likely sprang from two outrigger hulls being hitched together and lashed at an optimum distance apart, usually about 30% of their length, with struts high above the water and with a platform set between for extra space. When this occurred is guesswork, but it seems almost certainly to have been invented or in the last stages of invention when the proto-Polynesians began their deep-sea migrations three or four thousand years ago. From there it would have developed on its own as a large sea-going craft, being refined over the centuries or over the millennia into a superb piece of maritime machinery, as worthy to be compared with its fellow vessels as the clipper was to other Atlantic sailing ships; in short, a work of art.

*   *   *

"—their was four double Canoes went from this little Town and one from the west end of the Island Joind them—the canoes appeared to be about thirty foot long and about four foot Broad and three or three and a half foot Deep—they are built out of several small planks which are sewed together, and pind or trinld to several small Timbers not unlyke the frame of our Boats—their Manner of Sailing is this they Bring two allongside of one Another and lays their Beam Across the two, one a Midships in which they Step their Mast and one fored and Another Aft—and the whole is well lashd to the Gunwals of both canoes, this prevents them from oversetting when they Sail allong, they were lashd about three foot asunder, and the Mast stept in the Middle of the Midship beam which is supported with a pair of Shrouds and the halliards was belade closs aft, the Sail lookt lyke a topmast steeringsail with the Tack part Uppermost."—*George Robertson, 1767*

(Hugh Carrington, editor of Robertson's Journal, estimates these canoes at 10 ton.)

*   *   *

Once the main traditions had taken shape, the design as a whole must have existed full-blown in the mind of the *tahuna* before even the first chip flew from the first adze to strike. It is always so with an artist, a master builder. And yet it was more likely "full-blown" in general design than in particular, for no two boats, even though built to the most precise plans and specifications that modern man has devised and duplicated, have ever turned out to be the same; much less two horizontally floating canoe hulls, visualized in two vertically growing tree trunks. There are always unpredictables, and it is these that determine the end being . . . for better, for worse.

We can be reasonably sure, however, that every canoe started off in much the the same manner; differences being mostly of degree or importance related to the size rather than the kind.

First off the tree was selected, the basic dugout that formed the section we would call the keel and lower strakes, the backbone of the canoe. For an important chief this tree or a number of likely candidates were often chosen a generation or two before the contemplated felling. A good straight, sturdy tree was found in the forest and the brush around it was cleared away. Neighboring trees were probably left in place to encourage straight tall growth rather than branching. This clearing marked it as *tapu*, a chief's chosen tree and also reduced the vegetative competition. Such trees might be left in place for many decades. Sometimes they were scarred by peeling the bark on the side most vulnerable to the weather. This would cause a wound whose deadwood would decay and soften over the years so that in time the scooping out of the upper portion of the canoe would be easier; meanwhile the remaining three quarters of the circumferential wood would be strengthened by the stresses of weather and time. This was an ingenious way of asking the natural forces of your environment to assist you in the building of your canoe; and it took a bit of foresight.

The species of tree chosen varied, of course, from island group and even from island to island. Breadfruit was a favorite because it is more repulsive to the teredo worm than most woods. Its grain is twisty and its weight light. *Miro* makes one of the best, but it was often least accessible. The *tamanu* makes a good hull; though it is heavy, it is strong and thus resistant to wear on the beach or rocks or coral. The *purau* is light and soft, easily worked, good for small canoes and the wood par excellence for outrigger floats but relatively perishable. The great *kauri* pines of Maoriland were ideal of all trees, but they are limited, of course, to New Zealand and are thus johnny-come-latelies to canoe-making. They were used principally for the huge single-hulled war canoes which evolved after the double-hulled migration canoes had become obsolete. In such atoll groups as the Tuamotus *tou* and *tamanu* were used mostly, and in Micronesia almost any wood in those wood-scarce islands was used, patched and sewn together in incredibly crazy-quilt sections. And yet, sweet are the uses of adversity, these were the fastest and cleverest sailers of the whole ocean, in spite of the rumpled planes of their hull sides. And they attained very respectable sizes, too.

Many kinds of trees were used and the Polynesian woods were many. Of one thing you can be sure: the best woods were always used for their most suitable purposes. These people knew their woods with an intimacy and appreciation (or disgust) as few peoples in this world have known them. What could give you a better acquaintance than chipping away with a stone adze at the same old log for a whole solstitial season?

At length the time would come when the chief would tell his master craftsman to commence proceedings. There would be plenty of time; probably at least a year, perhaps two or three. Even if a tribe was conquered in warfare, its leaders were often given a year or so of grace to build canoes to seek a new dwelling place over the seas. Even an ambitious younger son who could not inherit land, a disappointed, jealous, or abductive lover, a social offender who had been banished, could take his time. The most insistent ejector of all, overpopulation, was perhaps the most leisurely one, though its gradually built-up pressures usually lay behind the more dramatic and immediate departures. Often great canoes were built in anticipation of such propellants; a sort of insurance against them. In such cases the canoes were taken apart and stored for the ultimate emergency.

At any rate a canoe was rarely if ever built in haste. It could not be: it took time, lots of it. And time is beneficial, perhaps essential, to maritime design.

So, in the company of the chief and his advisers and participants, the *tahuna* or master craftsman would first select the crucial tree. Every large canoe was a communal undertaking. Different families owned different parts, contributing to their initial manufacture, guarding and preserving them, each hanging his piece or pieces from the rafters of his house when the canoe was dismantled, ready whenever the high chief's summons came to bring them to the beach to be assembled.

Before any commencement of work there would have been a clear understanding about reward for the labor. This was largely a matter of food, as it was in *tatuing* and house-building, with additional compensation to the master in fine mats and tapa cloth. There was also the question in canoe-building of erecting a temporary shelter in the forest and supplying food on the spot. Once such an undertaking was started, it is probable that the workers kept at it constantly and that such distractions as women were forbidden. Because they ceased soon after our arrival, we know relatively little of the ceremonies and customs of the building of large canoes, but they most likely followed the similarly strict patterns that governed the two other great social enterprises; house-building and *tatu*. The quality of the food, the frequency of the feasts, additional compensation in mats and pigs and, above all the independence of the master and his workmen from any interference or even suggestion, perhaps even observation, by the commissioning chief or his intimates were all discussed in detail and agreed upon in accordance with ancient tradition in every particular beforehand. If the owner did not live up to his promises, the work would often stop, and so strong was custom that it could not be resumed by another party. The control of the "labor leader" (in this case both master designer and job boss combined) within his sphere was absolute. There was thus a curious balance between skill on the one hand and hereditary chieftainship on the other. Paramount though he was, there were limits to the power of the greatest chief.

These limits lay not, of course, in the relative strengths of the individuals, the *arii* on the one hand and the *tahuna* on the other, but rather in the sway of what we might call religion but what in Polynesia might better be termed custom, convention, or tradition. Every step was dictated by age-old integrated ceremony and this dictation, presided over by the godlike ancestors, might readily offset the temporal authority of the chief. They lived with their dead much more comfortably and respectfully than we do.

The first steps were ceremonial. The *tahuna* would go to the forest in the early evening and recite incantations to the chosen tree and to all the spirits that might become involved in the fate of the projected canoe. He would watch carefully for omens, good or ill, the approach and actions of birds, the moods of the weather, accidental arrivals of strangers, and the mysterious sounds of the forest. All of these would be messages from ancestral spirits, benign or malignant, and only the most augustly intuitive *tahuna* could read them aright.

If they proved auspicious, he would return to his band of workmen and they would all take their adzes, freshly sharpened, to the *marae* and lay them there in a *tapu* place to sleep for the night. In the morning they would awaken them and take them to the ocean to be bathed in the sacred water of *Moana*, the mother of all life. Only then would the adzemen be ready to walk up into the forested hills to start work.

War Canoes

War canoes may seem to have little pertinence to a discussion of long-range seafaring, but their construction must have derived in many respects from their predecessors, the great ocean-going vessels that brought their ancestors to the islands in the first place. Otherwise how could they have made war and the canoes in which to make it?

When Europeans arrived and gave us the first records of maritime invention, the migratory canoes had long since disintegrated. They had become obsolete, but their descendants, the war canoes, were everywhere in abundance. And so from the look of their hulls and the ingenuity of their construction we can perhaps get some appreciation of their antecedents.

The earliest is Tasman's, which Hornell says is a Maori war canoe from New Zealand. It is a puzzler because it bears no resemblance to any other recorded Maori canoe and it is about the only double canoe ever reported from New Zealand. One is tempted to dismiss it as an aberration, but Tasman's drawings of Tongan tongiaki *are remarkably accurate, so why would he have invented this strange craft? Although non-Maori in character, it does bear a resemblance to Cook Island vessels and there are many echoes in Cook Island and Maori art. Of course the Maori are believed to have reached their homeland by way of Rarotonga, so that is perhaps not so strange after all. If so, this might be termed a piece of evidence in the mysteries of Polynesian migrations.*

John Hawkesworth was a writer of notable prestige in his time who took a special interest in exploratory voyages, His three-volume account of the exploits of Wallis, Byron, Carteret, and Cook is handsomely though not always accurately illustrated.

This is a rather fanciful illustration from Hawkesworth showing the attack on the Dolphin which George Robertson on page 81 has left to the "pen of Milton" to describe. Here, as is to be expected of second-hand, stay-at-home reporting, the large double war canoe is being paddled stern forward and the upturned "bows" have curves and curls that never existed in Polynesia. Flags also were unknown. Where did that canopy come from and are the rowers all wearing Turkish turbans?

Hodges on the next two pages has left us by far the best record of war canoes and they come very probably from the one encounter at Pare, April 26, 1774, when Cook writes that there were "upwards of three hundred of them all rainged in good order for some distance along the Shore all Compleatly equip'd and Man'd." These pictures show the stages leading up to (or perhaps down to) the final published illustration. First is the impression from afar of the fleet as a whole. Then comes a detail of the command canoe, followed by a close-up wash drawing probably executed later aboardship in Tahiti. Later still in London the oil painting discards the flat bow and the huge stern with its large awkward Y, although it can be seen inconspicuously in the background. Perhaps he has just maneuvered the vessels about. Finally the published engraving on page 71 is reasonably faithful to the somewhat unfaithful painting. A splendid plan of a great war canoe draughted by Cook himself can be seen in the section on Plans.

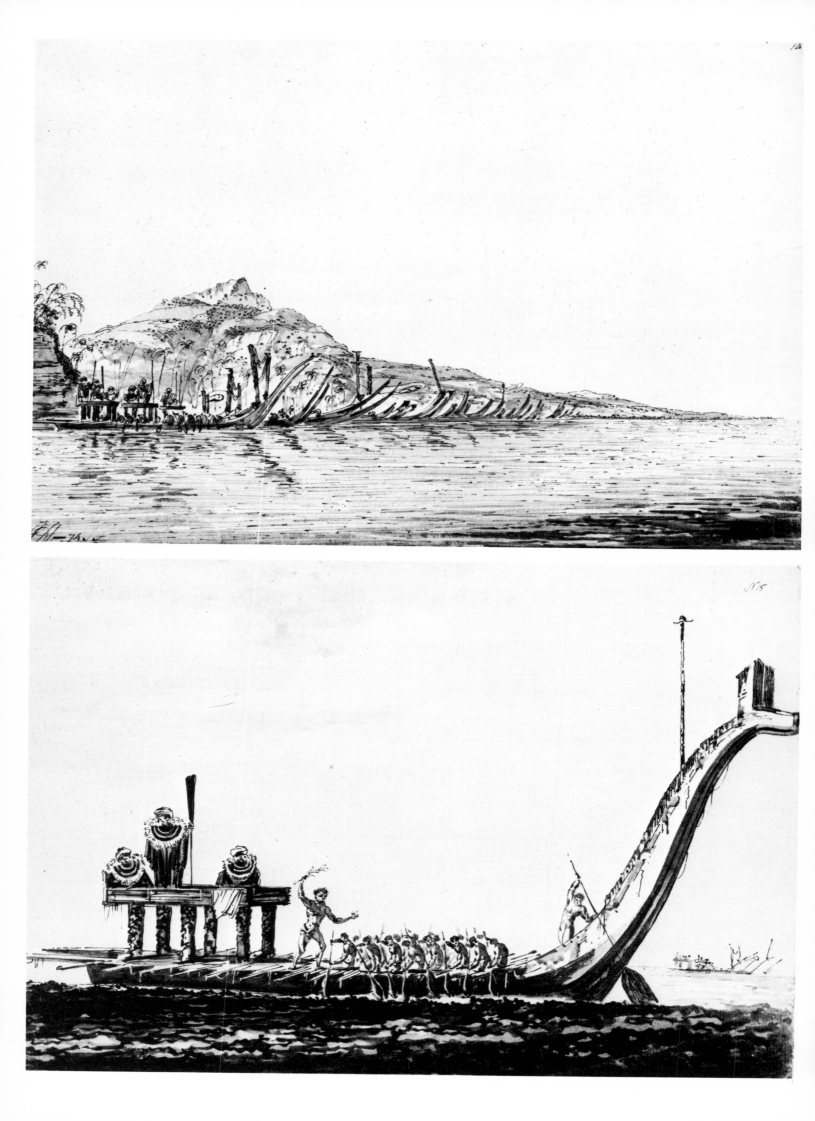

Although man's first tools were probably weapons, the most significant early tool to emerge was the adze. Every stone-age culture developed the adze, each in its own characteristic shape. The Polynesian chose the adze as his implement above all others and he developed it with care and tradition and skill. Perhaps no other man cared to attempt so much with it; perhaps other men found metal before they tried to do so. At any rate it seems safe to say that the Polynesians lived more lovingly with the adze than any other stone-age people.

When stone is the best material available for tools, then the adze is the best of tools, whether for sculpting a statue or for shaping a canoe hull. Even today the metal adze is used for this purpose in Polynesia. Elsewhere the adze is seldom seen now, so seldom that few people even know what it is. Ten thousand years ago it was probably the commonest of household tools. The adze was even more familiar to our ancestors than its offspring, the axe, is to us. To a modern, it is best described as an axe with the head or blade set at right angles to the haft or handle instead of parallel. Although it was the universal tool to stone-age man, it became supplanted by the metal axe which is quicker and more versatile, especially at cutting off limbs and heads. For shaping wood, a patient occupation, the stone adze was more accurate, more easily controlled and thus capable of more subtle work. There was developed for special uses an in-between tool, the side-hafted adze, a sort of cross between an adze and an axe, which is particularly effective in the inner sections of canoes. The axe is almost worthless for canoe work and it was from canoe making of course that the Polynesian's highest crafts and therefore his highest art were bred.

Adzes have been found all over the world, hundreds and hundreds of thousands of them. They are all made from hard stone; basalt, flint, argillite, obsidian etc. with one exception occurring probably only in Polynesia, the shell adze on coral atolls usually made from the giant tridacna clam. This is perhaps the only inhabitable environment in the world where stone is entirely lacking, but even here some trading was done with volcanic islands and imported basalt adzes are occasionally found.

The proportion of an adze's weight to a man's working strength finds a natural range; for heavy work about eight pounds, for light cutting a pound or so, lighter than that usually requires a chisel. For the medium range where most work is done, such as hollowing out a canoe log or felling a tree, an adze, like an axe, should weigh about three pounds. This right amount of stone to gain an efficient cutting edge, whose bevel must be much more obtuse than a metal tool, and to provide a tang for lashing, almost finds its own shape. The outside curve of that shape is, sensibly, the same arc that a man's arm takes in swinging the tool to its work. The other aspects of the shape of an adze head are, however, a very different matter. Whether it shall be quadrangular, triangular, oval, trapezoidal, or round in section, what flare of blade, what angle of bevel are all questions of utmost importance, not so much for the efficacy of the tool as for the gods, the ancestors, and the toolmaker's sense of eternal rightness.

*　　　*　　　*

A tii a naonao i te toi,		Go and dig out the adze
I te rua toi i Havaii;		In the adze pit in Havaii
E naoa, e iritia uruuru hia,		Hold, that it be taken out enchanted,
E pepee hia, ia hoa hia		Made light; that it may shoot sparks
I te haa tua mea.		In doing its work
I faaina hia i te one mata huahua;		It is whetted with fine sand;
I tavai hia i te one mata rii;		Made smooth with loose-grained sand;
I tapiri hia i te miro moa ma fau tu,		It is set in a firm handle of sacred miro,
E faua i te aha mata tini a Tane.		Bound with many-stranded sennit of Tane.
E raa te toi		The adze will become sacred
I te aha mata ioio a te tahua,		In the brilliant sennit of the artisan,
E u e mau		Which touches and holds
Ei maro	no te toi,	As a girdle for the adze,
Ei fafau	no te toi,	For the handle of the adze,
Te tua	no te toi,	The back of the adze,
Ei oiri	no te toi,	To make one the adze and the handle,
Ei mama	no te toi,	To make light the adze,
Ei taputapu	no te toi,	To consecrate the adze,
Ei tuitui	no te toi,	To impel the adze,
Ei faaoti	no te toi,	To complete the adze,
Ei ta mana	no te toi,	To give power to the adze.

*　　　*　　　*

After the incantation the *tahuna* would of course strike the first blow, commencing the scarfing of the trunk. Various techniques have been hypothesized, but records from Maori myths and chants seem the most detailed. Although practices differed, especially to accord with the size of the tree trunk, it seems likely that a common method was to cut two rather narrow horizontal channels a foot or two apart with short lateral strokes across the grain, using small adzes, and then to "scarf" out the wood between these channels with weighty down blows cutting with the grain with larger, heavier adzes.

The trunk was probably hewn, beaver-fashion, all around and guided to its desired direction of fall by strong guys of purau bark; ropes that had been made fast aloft before the cutting was very deep. Certainly they took pains to fell the tree where they wanted it, because the correct angle of descent was important to avoid shakes in the wood, hanging up, or splitting of large branches, and also to point the trimmed trunk in the direction of its destination on the shore. Sometimes fire was probably used to char the wood before adzing, but this may have been more prevalent in Maoriland, where the largest trees were used.

Once down, the ceremonies commenced again, first off perhaps with incantations and omens succeeded by another feast. Then the work of the rough shaping of the hull would be begun. In this stage many workmen could use their adzes together, but it was still a slow process. The outside of the hull was shaped first, then the log was set on its "keel" and the hollowing out started. Between sessions the log received some water to keep the grain alive and to prevent checking or premature drying. The hollow section holding water was covered with coconut fronds when work paused. Fire was probably used in many cases to char the

107

central wood before it was adzed out. But this was effective only in the mid sections. The ends would have to be cut more precisely from the beginning. This was done with side-hafted adzes whose blades were often broader, thinner, and more concave. They could, of course, be hafted either on the right or left and the angles of the blades changed for their particular purposes by their lashing to the haft.

In our culture a shipwright's tools, dealing as they do almost exclusively with curves and bevels, are strange objects to the conventional bench carpenter. Our shipwright employs a great variety of flex-bottomed planes, curved spoke shaves, rounded rabbeting planes, gouges, skew chisels, etc. The Polynesian used the same basic adze blade (as indeed we use the same basic steel blade), but he changed the hafting to suit the work to be done at and for the moment. His stone blades, patiently chipped and ground, were all he had, and there may be some advantage for a fine craftsman to use the same tool. Picasso has said: "We need one tool to do one thing and we should limit ourselves to that tool. In that way the hand trains itself. It becomes supple and skillful, and that single tool brings with it a sense of measure that is reflected harmoniously in everything we do . . . Then, too, forcing yourself to use restricted means is the sort of restraint that liberates invention."

The shaping of the hull on the forest slope was rough and preliminary because there was always danger of injury in skidding and hauling the log down to its finishing shed on the shore of the lagoon. Ropes and rollers helped when necessary, but the main power was stout legs and strong backs.

The canoe shed was a structure that drew the attention and admiration of the early explorers, missionaries, and traders. It was large, perhaps the largest of all Polynesian buildings. Banks measured one that was 50 paces by 10 and 24 feet high (150 ft. x 30 ft. x 24 ft.) and noted that it was only "middling size." It was built to contain a sizable double canoe with room for the workers to move around the two long hulls spread to their destined distance apart. Headroom was needed to suspend from the rafters the upper canoe strakes as they were cut and shaped to fit each other and to fit in turn onto the basic keel member or members. Long slender poles were set in the ground to frame the sides of the house, then brought together at their tops to form the ridge. These ribs were then thatched as usual with coconut or pandanus right down to the ground or near it.

From D'Urville

The rough-hewn, hollowed-out logs were first set bottom-up on trestles and carefully shaped down, first with adzes and then with coral rasps. Further smoothing was usually done with sharkskin and final polishing with pumice. In Hawaii a black "paint" was applied and a shiny gum varnish, but in most central island groups a gummy outer coating sometimes mixed with red clay over the natural wood was probably most common. The early European visitors could scarcely believe that such fine surfaces could be achieved with the locally available tools and methods. They often write that the finishes exceeded in quality the finest work that could be done in European shipyards.

*   *   *

"Confidering the greatnefs of the work, and the beauty of the execution, it is aftonifhing how, without the knowledge of iron, without rule or compafs, with a ftone adze only, the leg or arm bone of a man fharpened for the purpofe of chifel, gouge and gimlet, with coral only and fand, they can carve fo neatly and finifh fo fmoothly; our moft ingenious workmen could not exceed them. To cut with fuch inftruments, out of the hardeft and most folid wood to form planks, not more than two out of a tree, and build veffels capable of carrying three hundred perfons, muft require such endlefs labour and perfeverance, as makes it wonderful how they fhould ever be finifhed."—*Captain James Wilson, 1799*

*   *   *

Canoes from Other Island Groups

Recordings of double canoes from island groups other than Tonga or the Societies are rare; even for Hawaii there is little to show from the early visitors. However, a number of the actual vessels have survived so that their distinctive characteristics are well known.

109

James Webber circa 1777 made this interesting wash drawing of a Cook Island double canoe from Mangaia. Its sterns are a trade mark of these islands. Do they not resemble the early Tasman rendering of a Maori war canoe on page 102?

Much later, in the early 1920s, Peter Buck (Te Rangi Hiroa) took this photograph of a double canoe in Atiu in the Cook Islands.

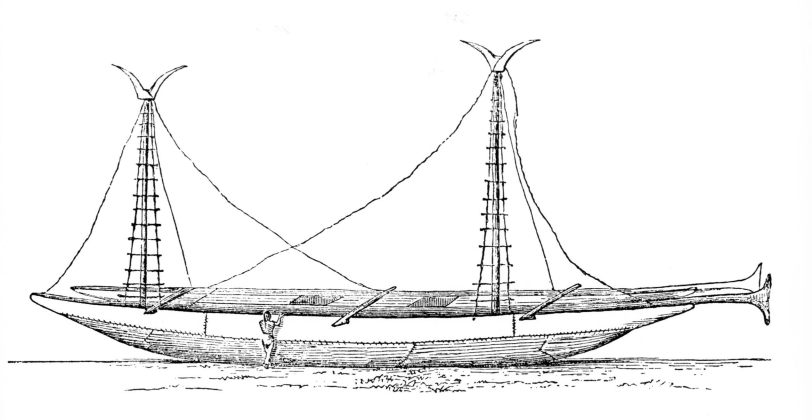

Commodore Wilkes on the United States Exploring Expedition of 1838-1842 recorded
these two double canoes from the Tuamotus. They should be compared with the Paris
plans on pages 148-151.

Captain Beechey of H.M.S. Blossom is responsible for this raft from the Gambier Islands, probably Mangareva. Double canoes abound in the legends of these islands, but rafts were the only means of water transport by the time the Europeans arrived.

This photograph, Hornell says, is of the last Samoan double canoe of the 'alia type. It was built for the German Kaiser, but its great size proved too difficult to transport it to Germany and it eventually just rotted on the beach.

This early field sketch by Webber of the well-known masked paddlers shows many constructional details of the Hawaiian double canoe. And the subsequent engraving shows how the engraver (or perhaps the artist himself) finished off the original, incidentally omitting two of the twelve rowers and thus altering the proportions of the canoe.

A CANOE of the SANDWICH ISLANDS, the ROWERS MASKED.

This is the original wash drawing in the Bishop Museum in Hawaii from which an engraving was made for Cook's Atlas. In the forward sailing canoe there appear to be 11

paddlers in each hull and 34 people on the center platform, a total of 56, which seems an extraordinary capacity for this size craft.

ÏEREOBOO, KING of OWYHEE, bringing PRESENTS to CAP.ᵗ COOK.

As it appeared in Cook's Atlas. An unusually faithful engraving, but notice that many men are holding their paddles in European rather than Polynesian fashion.

A field sketch by Webber of an Hawaiian canoe

The basic keel and garboard section was next set upright and the inside shaping was begun. This was usually not as sleek as the outside because there was of course no consideration of friction, but many beautifully fashioned interiors can be found, often with bulges remaindered, like pearls embedded in an oyster, to strengthen areas where knots occurred or where aberrant swirls of grain, rather than symmety of surface dictated the sweetest configuration. Ridges were sometimes left for lashing, for supporting thwarts, or for stiffening bilges. Ribs were very rarely used; the internal structure of the tree itself was strong enough. In very large canoes this bottom section was often fashioned of three pieces (sometimes, though infrequently, of two); a central section with bow and stern pieces fitted on each end with long, ingenious scarf joints.

Many old-time writers have been condescending about these pieced-together, "sewn" hulls, assuming that they would quickly work loose in heavy weather. I am convinced that such commentators have not known (and still do not) the tensile properties of wood when carved to the form of the natural growth of the grain. Nor have they appreciated the multiple resistant powers of those huge, cleverly angled scarf joints.

There is nothing stronger in wood than a hollow tree trunk. We know now that hollow spars built up from laminated woods are stronger than solid members. No ribs or fastenings were needed for these canoes; the grains and medullary rays of the wood, strengthened with a hundred years of stresses and strains from the winds, have a built-in, grown-in, live strength that surpasses any construction we have achieved until very recently. We have not been aware of it because we have not previously used it as the Polynesian shipwright did. Only in the last few decades have we begun to appreciate these strengths in laminated woods, plastics, and fiberglasses, all molded to forms inspired originally, as we now realize, by the inherent dynamics of the natural shapes of timber. And we have yet to find a material as supple and suitable to the sea.

The cross section of these large double-hulled sailing canoes was usually tapered into a keel to counteract leeway. Captain Wilson notes acutely, "the bottom is fharp; the fides rounding in towards the top in the midfhip frame, like the print of a fpade on a pack of cards."

When this fundamental keel- and garboard section was completed, the side planking and rails were fitted to it. These had been fashioned from flat boards or planks split from sections of tree trunk. The usual method was probably to cut a substantial section of log, to let an end be dried out in the sun or dry it with fire so that radial checks in the grain would show, then to open these up with wooden wedges, splitting off the side "slabs" until the widest and longest and soundest central planks could be obtained. This is much the same concept as our sawing except that splitting with the run of the grain results in a naturally stronger, sleeker piece of wood. This was split out at perhaps twice the desired thickness and then adzed down to suit. It might finally be a bit more wavy than our sawn boards, but that would not worry its passage through the water.

The edges were then squared and fitted to the keel portion. Actually none of the joints were squared in the sense we use this term. All shaping was done by eye; pare and try and pare again. There was never such a tool as a rule, straightedge, square, T-bevel or snap line. Geometry did not exist for the Polynesian; he never conceived of a carpenter's plane.

117

Joints were tested with blacking made from water and burnt coco fiber applied to smooth tapa cloth to mark high spots for further trimming, much as we now use carbon paper. Flaws or knots were cut out and patched.

From E. S. C. Handy

He lashed all of his joints. Many of the early European discoverers remark rather scornfully that his boats were sewn together, so perhaps we might compare his joinery with our tailoring where the expert cuts his gores and gussets guided by chalk largely by eye. But even this loose comparison is not good, for the Polynesian apparently never traced his design beforehand,* nor did he use templates or patterns; what he did was to address himself to each piece of wood and its individual characteristics as it came along. Its final shape was not determined without careful consideration of its own properties: its grain, knots, flaws, etc. The worker did this while suspending his plank from the roof rafters just over the upper edge of the base member and then chipped away at both edges of his joint until they fitted together to his satisfaction. The same method was used, of course, to fit the ends of his plank and then for the next one above it. Sometimes when a vessel was built of many pieces, the craftsmen must have had a sort of "mobile" dangling about them as they trimmed the shapes and edges to fall in place like a jigsaw puzzle. Here again there was no conventional symmetry, but the basic principle of juxtaposing vertical and horizontal joints to gain maximum strength resulted in roughly rectangular patterns. This would apply, however, only to the sides. On bow and stern fittings, where stresses were more complex, the angles became more complicated, especially in contriving the great scarf joints.

After the pieces were fitted to each other, the process of securing the joints was begun. First off the holes for the lashings were bored. Probably a pump drill was the most common instrument used, sometimes with a stone or coral momentum wheel, sometimes with a wooden one. Often, no doubt, a two-man drill was operated with one worker guiding and pressing while the other did the reciprocal spinning with a bow. Shell was probably the usual material for the drill point, and small shell chisels were used for making square holes. Occasionally a chip of flint or obsidian made a particularly durable point. If such holes had wide bevels, they were driven from both sides and where an extra thick joint occurred, from the top as well, but a surprisingly small, neat hole could be achieved with a narrow chisel.

*   *   *

"Girls came over and Traded with the Gunner for their Earrings which was pearls of a fine luster but all spoild in the boring, how they are able to bore pearls I know not, but I think its Impossible to do without some small metal Instrument, as no bone or shell can pearce a pearl, neather any kind of stone be brought to so fine a point, as to bore so small a hole as was in this pearls, for which reason I am almost certain they have some kind of metal but what kind it is I neaver was able to discover."—*George Robertson, 1767*

(Perhaps he had not thought of shark tooth.)

*   *   *

It was a painstaking process, all of it with many intervals to change drill points, sharpen adzes and chisels, sight and fit, shave and rasp. Their whole tempo of work must have been very different from that to which we are accustomed or to which we drive ourselves. But it must, all of it, also have fitted into much the same sort of rhythm, slow to us but second nature to them, so that they ate and talked and slept and fished and gathered coconuts; everything in the normal routine

---

*An exception should perhaps be noted for the art of *tatu* when indications of designs were sometimes traced beforehand with soft charcoal upon the skin. But these were probably not graphics to be followed in our sense; rather they were indications of old themes or motifs to be approved or rejected or modified by the patron chief.

Captain Wallis of the Dolphin, who "discovered" Tahiti in 1767, brought back this canoe from the Tuamotus, now in the British Museum, the oldest authentic Polynesian canoe in existence and a good example of "sewn" seams. It is 12½ feet long.

except making love, which was almost always *tapu* during these special under-takings. Could love making have been too distracting an interruption to the even pace of the whole endeavor?

All the while as they chipped their careful flakes of wood, slowly, slowly, they perceived the vision of the great canoe taking shape. With all of life beating at much the same pace, there would be little impatience, little urgency to get on with the job. This work would be fitted into the leisurely rhythm of a man's life; his life would not, as in our culture, be fitted to the demanding rhythm of the job. Perhaps that is why the Polynesian "progressed" so slowly; perhaps it is also why he remained so tenaciously human. Perhaps, on the other hand, he was just con-forming to the dictates of stone as opposed to steel.

After the holes were made, the lacing or lashing would be begun, although first there would be a spreading of breadfruit gum to "pay" the joint and a distribution of loose coconut fiber for what we would call oakum, to "caulk" the joint. But these comparisons are not accurate, for whereas their joints were always laid flat together, ours were V-shaped, with the oakum and pitch driven from outside in.

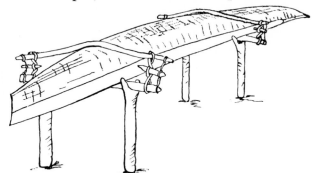

From Hornell

Thus ours were squeezed tight by the introduction of a filler; theirs were shaped tight, sealed and squeezed together with a torque or Spanish windlass (long before any Spaniards had seen their ocean). Guards made from strips of the spine of the coconut frond were then placed against the outside crack in the gluey breadfruit sap, and when the whole joint was snug, the lashing was passed through the holes, drawn up tight with a forked stick, secured with wooden pegs jamming it in each hole and then knotted on the inside as a precaution against the loosening of the pegs. Trying to describe this detailed procedure in words is awkward, but draw-ings make it reasonably clear, although one cannot possibly appreciate the fin-ished result without seeing it and running one's hand over the final joint itself.

There has been much skepticism about frail craft, sewn together, leaking pro-fusely and working loose in any kind of seaway. Such old sailor yarns (that might as well be called old wives' tales) are nonsense. The lashed joints of these great sea-going canoes were marvels of construction. Considering the lack of metal fastenings, they were far better than anything else of the kind ever devised. And even in comparison with our ship construction of many centuries later, they were equal in their effectiveness. They look frail to us, for we built great heavy hulls planked and ribbed and sheathed; massive things that for all their bulk all too often succumbed to stormy seas, dry rot, and teredo worms. We know now that bulk is no guarantee of safety; that huge steel hulls will twist and hogback when light cockleshells will ride the storm.

121

Canoe Models

As a review of Polynesian canoe types these models may be of some interest. They are early and were not made for tourists, but rather for ceremonial purposes, so they can probably be presumed to be authentic.

This old model of a Marquesan double canoe, Hornell says, is "probably the only one of its kind. The discontinuous line of shell inlay along the washstrake seam is a feature not recorded by any writer."

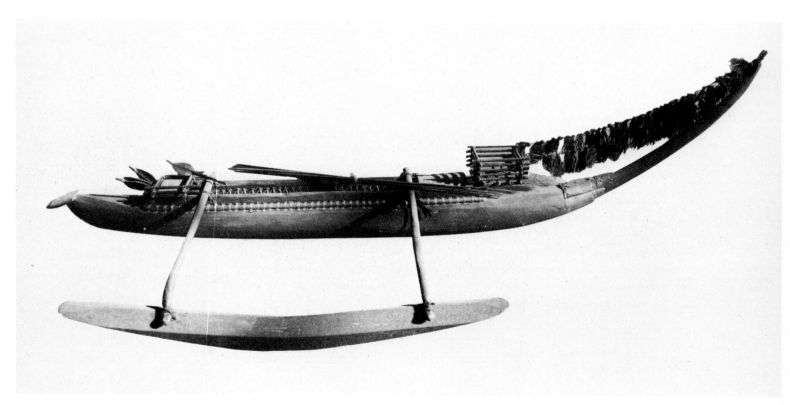

This one from the Marquesas in the collection of the Peabody Museum in Salem is the rarest and is considered by Hornell to be as good a representation of the old-time type as exists. The outrigger is probably not authentic.

This double sailing canoe from Manihiki shows from both windward and leeward sides how these canoes with sterns and bows reversed were designed to tack into the wind without coming about.

This Tuamotuan double sailing canoe shows the characteristic steering oar and the windward shelter that is reminiscent of Tongan and Fijian vessels two or three thousand miles to the westward.

Another Tuamotuan model was built by Admiral F. E. Paris from the plans of the full-scale canoe that appears on pages 148-149.

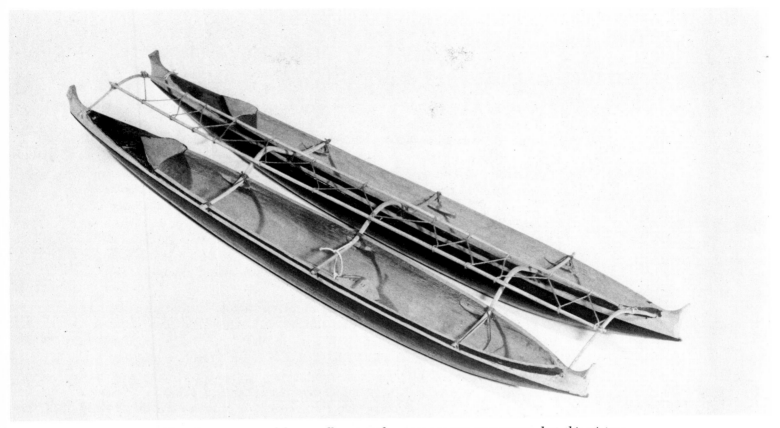

Hawaiian canoe models as well as actual canoes are not uncommon, but this picture shows well the structure of the struts and center platform that secured the two hulls together.

This Tongan canoe model has the same type of shelter, but it is proportionately much larger than the Tuamotu vessel.

Polynesian canoe construction is being appreciated more and more today as we experiment with straddle stability, in the use of catamarans and trimarans and new plastic techniques that hark back to the principles of the hollow tree trunk. Captains Cook, Bougainville, Vancouver and all may have thought these canoes fragile compared to their own sturdy vessels, but they had already performed greater feats than the ancestors of those captains had been able to accomplish.

Coconut fiber, or sennit or coir as it is alternately called, is one of the most durable of rope yarns in salt water; its lasting powers when wet and while wet are probably equal or superior to any other natural fiber. Its unstretchability is also remarkable; it has less give than manila, far less give than nylon. It wore out readily, but it was easily replaced even at sea. It was bountiful and cheap. And breadfruit gum is a most superior resin.

To be sure, all of these "sewn" vessels displayed a good deal of give and take in a heavy seaway, but flexibility is the life of a ship. A too-rigid construction will snap and founder; an elastic one will conform and float. That is why modern processed rubber is perhaps the ultimate material for short-term safety at sea.

Yes, those canoes did leak; all boats do; though these more than most. But there were bailers aplenty and one must always remember that these light wooden craft never sank. They could be filled with water by a fluky sea and swamped to their gunwales, but still they could be thrust fore and aft by swimmers and eventually bailed out dry; well, almost dry.

Serious leaking in our eighteenth-century ships would mean certain death if the pumps could not keep up with it, and today a power failure means the same inevitable disaster. We must realize that if leaking meant no more than extra effort, or repairs postponed or brought on by a piece of bad luck; if it meant a good wetting but rarely, almost never, certain death, we might develop a more tolerant attitude toward a leaky craft. After all, even a swamped canoe is a life raft.

But we would not compare for safety a vessel such as the *Endeavour* with a modern oceanographic explorer such as the *Chain.* Why then should we compare Polynesian migration canoes that were crossing long stretches of ocean before the birth of Christ with James Cook's ships nearly two thousand years later? We should not put these methods of construction and their relative safety or efficiency in competition. We should recognize the marvelous creation that this great double canoe was and appreciate its feats in carrying people, pigs, dogs, chickens, and a rich garden of fruits and vegetables to all the hundreds of inhabitable islands lifting out of the great south sea.

Once the canoe hulls were assembled and their surfaces finished, the cross struts that held them parallel to each other at the correct distance apart were lashed to their gunwales. Three or five or sometimes as many as twenty booms were laid across. These had been carefully cut and shaped in their characteristic reverse curves while the hull work was being completed. Each had its traditional proportions and the braided sennit lashings elaborately and decoratively seized everything together. Accessories such as platform gratings, shelter house members and roofings, masts, spars, rigging, sails of plaited matting, bailers, and paddles all lay ready to complete the craft.

But first, of course, must come the launching. This was the most transcendent, the culminating ceremony of them all. The whole community, meaning usually

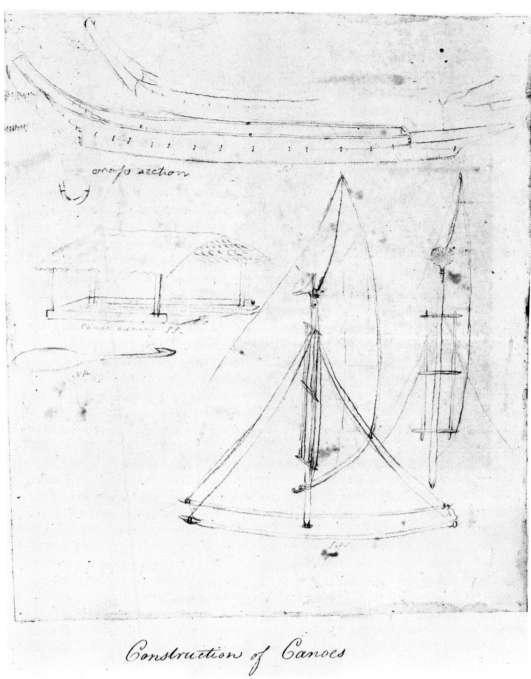

Construction of Canoes

Banks says a 32-foot boat bearing a 25-foot mast would be the "common proportion."

the entire populace of the district or groups of valleys that lay under the hereditary authority of the paramount chief or *arii* would have started preparations many days ahead, indeed choice pigs would have been designated and fattened for the occasion perhaps months in advance.

Commencing from the outlying areas a stream on foot of people, animals, chickens, and children would start winding their leisurely paths skirting the lagoon. Within greeting distances of them heavily laden canoes would glide along offshore, a procession of heaped-up burdens of foodstuffs: urus and taros, kumara, fei, sugarcane, melons, mountain apples; bananas, bananas; coconuts, coconuts; chestnuts and candlenuts; slathers of fish sliding in the bilges; lobsters and crabs, oysters and conches; a turtle or two exclusive for the chief, and baskets of slithery octopus and snails.

They would have started long before daybreak, lighting their way with torches, joking, laughing, singing, scolding as they walked in family clusters single file through the darkness or the pale moonlight. For the launching and the feast would probably coincide with the end of a waxing moon so that they could all travel pleasantly in the cool of the night to arrive at the place of preparations before the sun rose too high.

There they would dig the ovens for the feast, cut the firewood, grate the coconuts, marinate the raw fish in salt water, pound the sticky pois, plait the niau baskets, stick the squealing pigs and collect their spurting blood. At last the stones would be heated, the flaming embers drawn out, and the ovens filled with pigs and breadfruits, leaf packages of poi, big fish, little fish, shellfish, crayfish, and a red-gold ring of fei all around. Then it would be layered over with blue-green banana fronds, covered over again with old mats and lastly piled high with dirt.

Then would come a time to rest in the noonday heat, to joke and gossip and to play for a while, games of javelin tossing, quoits, stilts and archery, but mostly moe, moe, sleep and love in the sultry silent shade.

In midafternoon the community gradually comes alive. Preparations for the feast are renewed and preparations for the launching are completed. Then come incantations from the *tahuna* and orders from the chief. All rites are observed according to the ancient customs. Perhaps two human sacrifices are brought forth and laid out so that their bodies can act as rollers for the twin hulls. These are probably two misfits designated secretly long ago but only suddenly killed without warning. And all, except their close relations perhaps, will receive this sacrifice and appreciate the *mana* these two will give to the great canoe and the appeasement they will provide for the presiding gods and ancestral spirits.

Now the canoe, amidst great shouting, cheering, and singing, is hauled and pushed over its rollers, over its *tapu* corpses at a swiftly accelerating pace until it leaps forth from the shore and shoots out with a loud splash onto the shallow waters of the lagoon. At that moment its bows are pulled downward and its sterns are thrust upward so that it takes its first great sacred drink of the sea.

Thus "baptized," it is now given the name by which it will always hereafter be known and which may, if the canoe proves worthy, pass into legend and its fame go down through the generations.

Every subtlest feature of this whole procedure is minutely scrutinized by the chief and the *tahuna* and keenly noticed by all the observers and participants. Each occurrence, whether adventitious such as the arrival of a bird or a change in the weather, or accidental such as a stumble by one of the pushers, and each item of behavior such as the disgruntlement of one of the pullers or the failure of a log to roll, most important of all the behavior of the canoe in the water as it settles to its final trim, everything of this sort is an omen, and the sum of these omens is the fate of the canoe.

If they are propitious, well and good, the proper verses are chanted and rejoicing is general. But so powerful are these signs and portents that if they are sufficiently contrary, the canoe may even be hauled ashore and destroyed.

Usually with blessings and forebodings mixed, the hulls ride out on the waves to be paddled about for a while and then either anchored in the lagoon for the night or drawn back into the shed to await the start of the rigging tomorrow.

The ovens have meanwhile been opened and the feast is on.

grave par Croissy

Canot de l'Isle Taiti à la Voile.

Single-Hull Outrigger Canoes

So far, these pictures have shown double canoes almost exclusively because these were the sea-going vessels that made their way by the stars. Logically this book should be restricted to them, but since so many of them had disappeared before the European came to record them, this section on single-hull outriggers is included. Although quite different in sailing characteristics, they have similarities in hull construction, sails, and rigging and therefore probably shed some light on their antecedents and former contemporaries, the double hulls. This is particularly important in the case of the Marquesans who may have been the first settlers of eastern Polynesia and thus the first to abandon the old long-voyage craft and to concentrate, as did all the other island groups, on the far more numerous and varied single hulls for offshore and interisland travel.

The first recording of a canoe in the Society Islands was this engraving from Bougain-ville's account of his visit in Tahiti, shortly after Wallis but before Cook. The outrigger attachments are carelessly and inaccurately shown and the leeside runout has a false cupping, but the sail, bow, and stern are all genuine Polynesia. What is that calabash doing at the top of the mast? It occurs and recurs in depictions of Tahitian canoes. It also occurs and recurs in tatu designs where it may be a symbol of the womb. There is no maritime function that could be attributed to it. It seems surely that it must be decorative or magical or what we might call religious.

These two drawings by Webber of a Tahitian outrigger are another example of a quick, rough field sketch later refined into a careful wash drawing, and they show well the construction of what was probably the commonest canoe hull of all.

Hodges, Tahiti above, Tonga below.

There are very few records of canoes from the Marquesas and none, except a model, of a double canoe. They did not differ greatly and yet they had their distinct characteristics, especially the recurved stern. Whether those three decorative symbols on the bow were genuine or an invention of the London engraver seems dubious. The early sketch and later painting show no sign of them. The engraver has gratuitously added a spiral tatu to one canoeist's buttock, a motif that could not occur except in Maoriland three thousand miles away. Hornell says that this is the only recording of a Marquesan sail.

This sketch of a canoe in Nukuhiva is interesting because it shows in some detail the elaborate outrigger attachments characteristic of Marquesan craft. It also demonstrates how much heavier and sturdier they were than other Polynesian vessels. They had to be because there is no coral, no lagoons in these islands. They had to be put directly to sea.

This engraving of a Marquesan canoe from Langsdorff gives a general idea of the shape of the vessel but misses the whole purpose of the outrigger.

Webber drew this outrigger in Tonga with attachments reminiscent of the Marquesas.

Dumont D'Urville was also the earliest to give us a record of a Samoan canoe, somewhat crude and clumsy by Society or Tuamotuan standards.

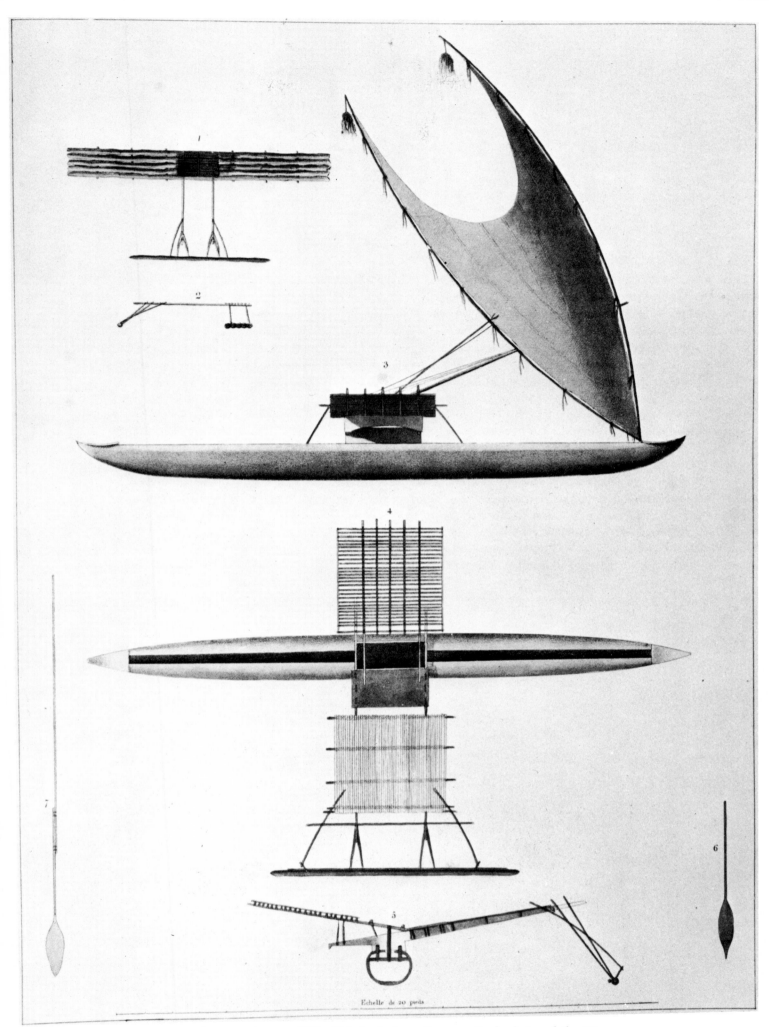

This rendering in Dumont D'Urville's book shows how cunningly designed the Micro-nesian sailing craft were. The whole was a beautifully balanced sailing machine the like of which for efficiency has subsequently never been equaled.

Rigging and Seamanship

The details and manner of rigging are better described in pictures than in words. All the material, needless to say, came from trees. Masts probably from toa (ironwood, *casuarina*) for strength; spars from purau and even bamboo for lightness; sails were mats woven from pandanus leaves; lashings and lines were usually sennit, though in many cases purau bark, which is so easily stripped, shreds so readily lengthwise, but is so incredibly tough to break when fresh, was often used for seizings, lashings, and even for anchor rode. Cook notes "some of the rope necessary for rigging of these vessels is 4 or 5 inches thick and made exactly like ours." Probably this was made from *hau* (hibiscus), or it might have been coconut fiber.

*   *   *

"In navigating their double canoes, the natives frequently use two sails, but in their single vessels only one. The masts are moveable, and only are raised when the sails are used. They are slightly fixed upon a step placed across the canoe, and fastened by strong ropes or braces extending to both sides, and to the stem and stern. The sails were made with the leaves of the pandanus split into thin strips, neatly woven into a kind of matting. The shape of the sails of the island-canoes is singular, the side attached to the mast is straight, the outer part resembling the section of an oval, cut in the longest direction. The other sails are commonly used

Sketch by Webber

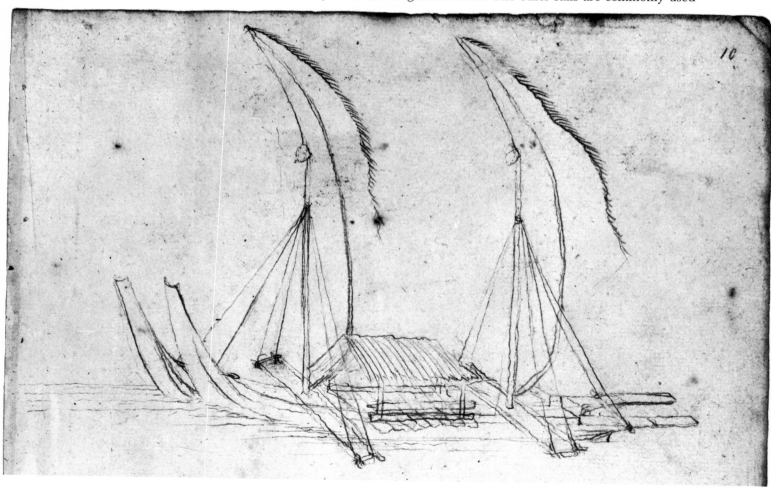

in the same manner as sprit or lugger sails are used in European boats. The ropes from the corners of the sails are not usually fastened, but held in the hands of the natives. The rigging is neither varied nor complex; the cordage is made with the twisted bark of the hibiscus, or the fibres of the cocoanut husk—of which a very good coiar rope is manufactured."—*William Ellis, 1829*

*   *   *

In considering cordage it is interesting to note that no evidence has been found in Polynesia of anything but simple knotting. Of course all archaeological remains of this sort are sadly perishable, but even in the extensive assembly of knots at the Bishop Museum, nothing turns up that resembles a bowline or even a fisherman's bend; they are all simple clove and half hitches, lark's-heads, square knots, sheet bends, or weaver's knots. When the elaborate and ingenious weaving, plaiting, basketry, and net making is studied; when the foundations of Hawaiian helmets are examined; and when intricate cat's cradles are unraveled, there seems no question that these people were capable of devising complex knottings. Why did these master seamen display so little of what is considered by us a sophisticated phase of seamanship? One possible explanation is that they felt little need for elaborate knots. These have been devised by us over the centuries for a basically economic purpose; to preserve our precious rope so that the knot can be untied and the rope used again. No such incentive moved the Polynesian. There was always plenty of purau bark and plenty of coconut sennit ready to hand. It was easier to throw an old knotted rope away and lay hold of a new one than to bother with a bowline, a carrick bend, or a Turk's-head. He did well at splicing and his decorative desires led him to labyrinthine lashings both afloat and ashore rather than to complicated knottings of rigging.

Another possible factor is time on the sailor's hands. It seems likely that the Polynesian at sea had less leisure than the European. In the first place his voyages were considerably shorter. His quarters were more confined and his duties probably less intermittent. There were always bailing and paddling in addition to the usual maritime exigencies such as trimming sail, steering, cleaning, repairing, eating, sleeping, and lookout. Idle time, so significant a factor on our long ocean voyages often of several years' duration, was probably not even a noticeable one on his; and hence no bell ropes or eye splices, Mattie Walkers, monkey's fists, or grommets. Idle time ashore, that he had in plenty, you might say in plethora, and hence those great stone tikis patiently pecked and also those wooden canoes patiently chipped and polished.

All of which leads, perhaps roundaboutly, to the art or practice of being a Polynesian seaman or of handling a Polynesian vessel at sea. There is much evidence, legendary as well as practical, that this was a highly specialized performance, just as our European maritime organization has always been. It does not seem that they had a captain, a commander supreme in all respects as we have usually had. There was rather a dual command: the chief who owned the canoe and who by hereditary rights had paramount power but who was subject to the specialized knowledge and metaphysical prowess of the *tahuna* or master of navigation. Theoretically the chief could override his council, but he did so at the peril not only of discrediting his mortal maestro but also of offending the immortal gods and spirits of whom the *tahuna* was the representative and from whom (presumably) he had received his supernal instructions. So things were probably a bit more complicated for the Polynesian master than they were for Captain Cook or Captain Ahab. They, however, are of a later and perhaps more fortunate generation. Europeans before them such as Mendana and Quiros, Schouten and Le Maire, were accustomed to a dichotomy of command. Thereafter the ranks in a canoe were probably dictated by the customary rigors facing a small boatload of men on a large expanse of water. The men at the steering paddle were of higher order than our quartermasters, more comparable perhaps to mates. Paddlers no doubt had precedence

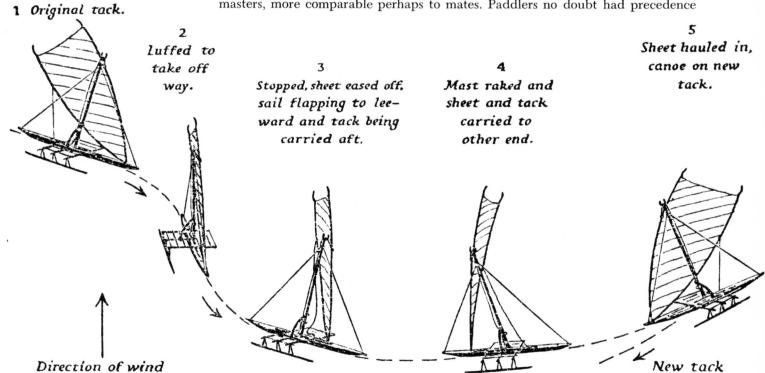

1 Original tack.

2 luffed to take off way.

3 Stopped, sheet eased off, sail flapping to leeward and tack being carried aft.

4 Mast raked and sheet and tack carried to other end.

5 Sheet hauled in, canoe on new tack.

Direction of wind

New tack

Most Polynesian canoes were "tacked" into the wind by shifting the mast or the sprit sail, thus reversing the bows and sterns. See the Manihiki model on page 123.

Since the purpose of the outrigger or "float" of a sailing canoe is to balance with its weight rather than its buoyancy, it must be kept to windward at all times; otherwise it would sink and break off when a puff of wind heeled the boat over. Most canoes are double-ended, with the mast stepped in the center so the tack or foot of the sail is transferred from one end of the boat to the other. The vessel does not "come about" as we do, but instead is reversed to shift from starboard to port tack. Based on Grimble.

over bailers, with sail handlers somewhere between, but there may easily have been much trading about to take turns at different activities. It is a good guess, however, that judging from the way Polynesian seamen function today and indeed from the way all seamen tend to function everywhere, that every man had his job and that by and large he stuck to it.

These comparisons when they are listed out seem routine enough and perhaps hardly worth noting. But this is not true of Polynesian seamanship as a whole. It did (and still does on outriggers especially) require a special set of skills that can find comparison only in our esoteric yacht racing teams. A man's weight counted significantly in times of stress or manuever. He had to be in the right spot at the right moment and he had to hop to it to be there, particularly when tacking into the wind or when heeled over by a sudden gust. He must needs scramble up his ladder mast, dance about on struts, and swing out on shrouds to keep his craft in balance, and all this was a very important part of his function. In other words he had to be a gymnast as well as a seaman. Ellis likens the acrobatics of a canoe to a bird flying, counterpoising its wings and feathers, its weights and tail flicks. Sometimes for the sport of it they would fly a huge kite to speed their bonny boats over the rippling waters of the lagoon.

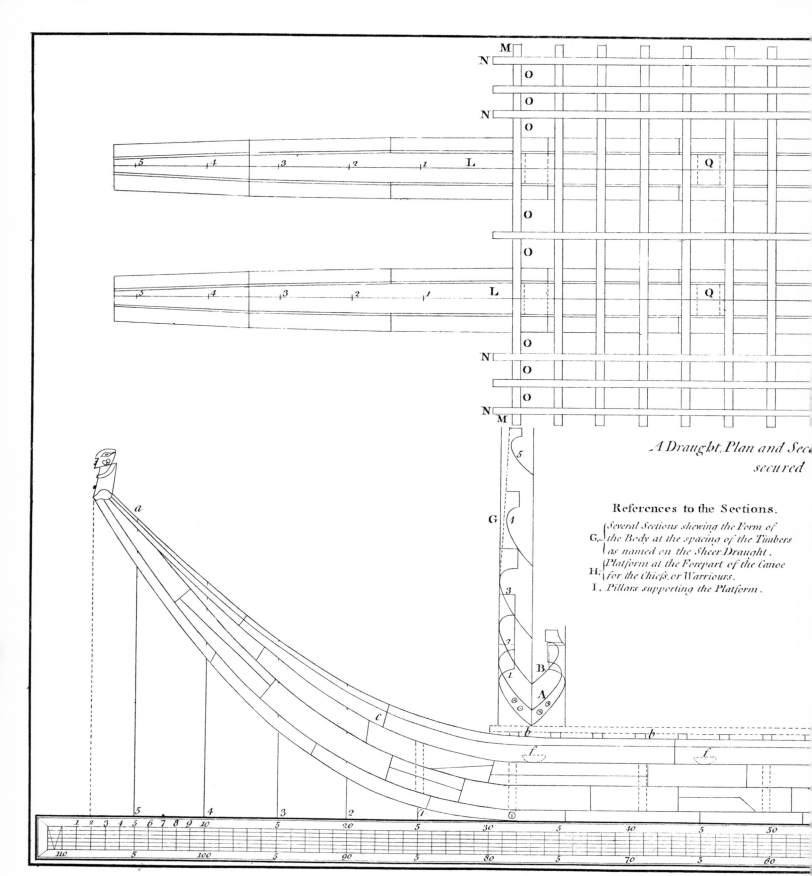

A Draught, Plan and Sec...
secured

References to the Sections.

G. ⎰ Several Sections shewing the Form of
⎱ the Body at the spacing of the Timbers
as named on the Sheer Draught.

H. ⎰ Platform at the Forepart of the Canoe
⎱ for the Chiefs, or Warriours.

I. Pillars supporting the Platform.

Plans o

The plans on these and the following fourteen pages are self explanatory to anyone
acquainted with drawings of this sort and will be given only identification by island
groups with conversions of the scales from meters to feet.

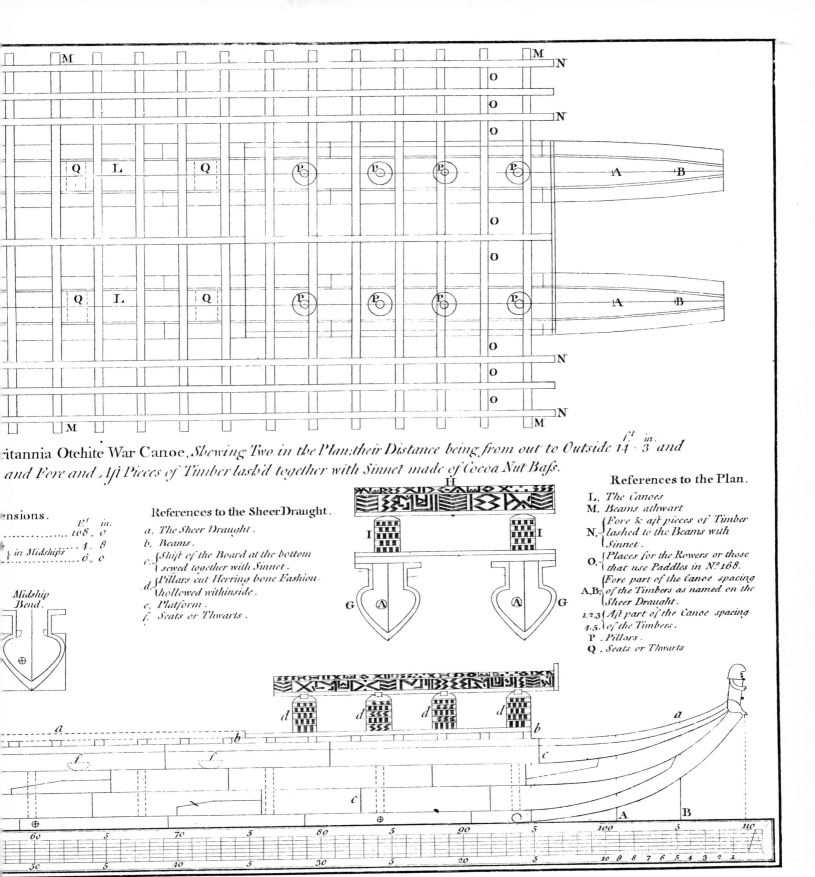

itannia Otehite War Canoe. *Shewing Two in the Plan; their Distance being from out to Outside* 14 $^{f.t}$ 3 $^{in.}$ *and*
and Fore and Aft Pieces of Timber lash'd together with Sinnet made of Cocoa Nut Bass.

		ft.	in.
ensions.		108	0
in Midships		4	8
		6	0

Midship Bend

References to the Sheer Draught.

a. The Sheer Draught.
b. Beams.
c. Shift of the Board at the bottom sewed together with Sinnet.
d. Pillars cut Herring bone Fashion. hollowed within side.
e. Platform.
f. Seats or Thwarts.

References to the Plan.

L. The Canoes
M. Beams athwart
N. Fore & aft pieces of Timber lashed to the Beams with Sinnet.
O. Places for the Rowers or those that use Paddles in N°.168.
A,B. Fore part of the Canoe spacing of the Timbers as named on the Sheer Draught.
1.2.3 Aft part of the Canoe spacing 4.5. of the Timbers.
P. Pillars.
Q. Seats or Thwarts.

Canoes

This first is a nearly full size reproduction of the original published edition of what is probably the most famous plan of all, Captain Cook's record of a Tahitian war canoe, the longest vessel accurately recorded in early Polynesia, 108 feet.

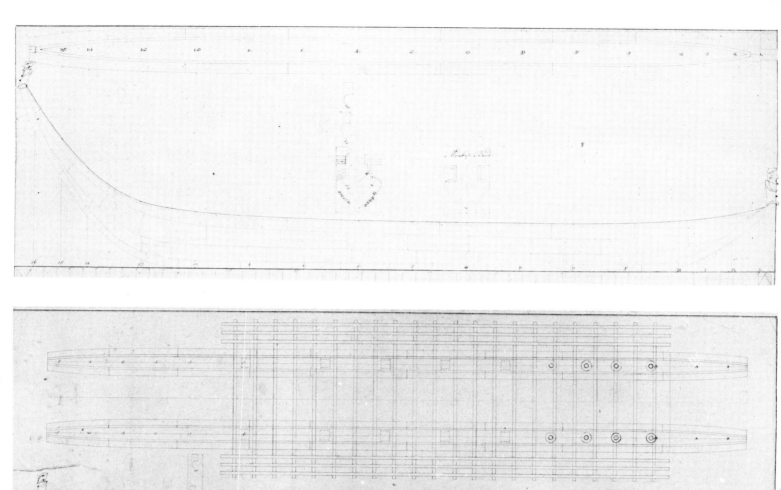

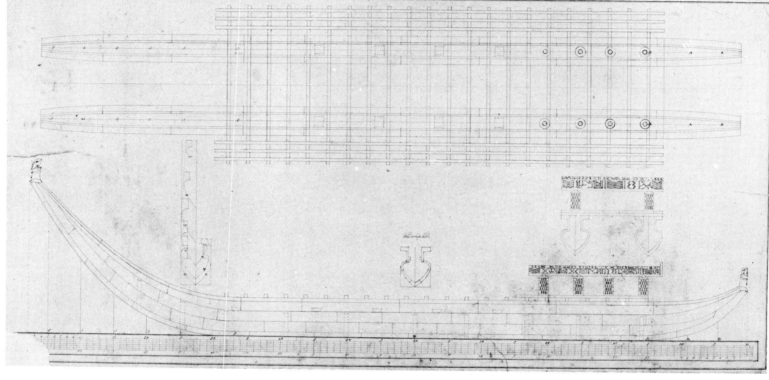

The plans on this page are Cook's and very likely by his own hand. The two preliminary sketches, hitherto unpublished, are originals from the collection of Admiral Isaac Smith now in the Mitchell Library in Sydney. The bottom is a reproduction of the final, printed in Cook's Atlas. The middle one is clearly an early version and the top one appears to be a still earlier draught of one of the canoe hulls, but there seem to be differences in proportions and details.

On the next page Cook's tongiaki from "Amsterdam," as Tonga was first known, is 69 feet. The small outrigger canoe in the original plan has been removed.

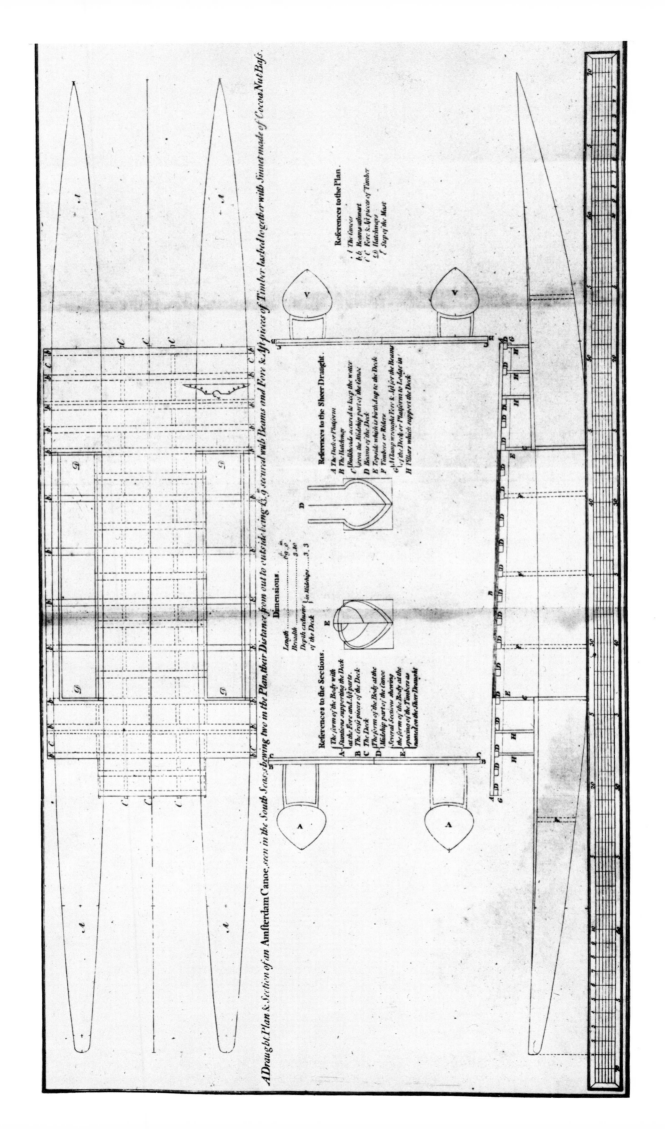

A Draught, Plan & Section of an Amsterdam Canoe, seen in the South Seas; shewing two in the Plan, their Distance from out to outside being 5.9 secured with Beams and Fore & Aft pieces of Timber lashed together with Sinnet made of Cocoa Nut Bals.

Dimensions.
	ft. in.
Length	69.0
Breadth	3.10
Depth exclusive of the Deck in midships	3. 3

References to the Sections.

A— The form of the Body with Stantions supporting the Deck at the Fore and Aft parts.
B— The Crossi piece of the Deck
C— The Deck
D— The form of the Body at the Midship part of the Canoe
E— The form of the Body at the Several Section shewing the form of the Timbers at the Several Section & the spacing of the Timbers as mark'd on the Sheer Draught

References to the Sheer Draught.

A The Deck or Platform
B The Hatchway
C Bulkheads secured to keep the water from the Midship part of the Canoe
D Beams of the Deck
E Topside which is birth'd up to the Deck
F Timbers or Riders
G A Clamp wrought Fore & Aft of the Beams of the Deck or Platform to Ledge in with Deck or Platform to Ledge in
H Pillars which support the Deck

References to the Plan.

A The Canoe
b.b Beams athwart
C C Fore & Aft pieces of Timber
D Hatchways
E Step of the Mast

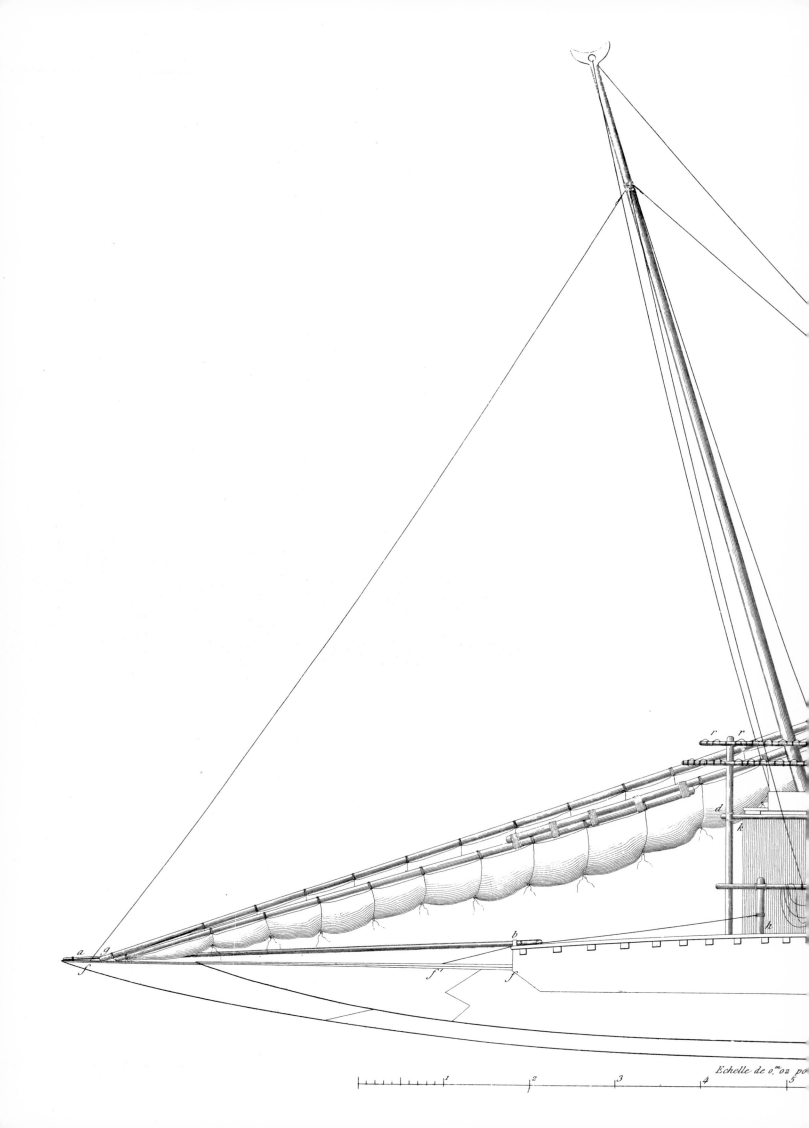

All the other plans, with the exception of Langsdorff's draught of a Marquesan out-rigger, are the work of Admiral F. E. Paris, who sailed with Dumont D'Urville on the Astrolabe 1826-1829. They were taken from his large folio volume (14 x 21 in.) pub-lished in 1843 as an "Atlas" to his Essai sur la Construction Navale des Peuples Extra-Européens ou Collection des Navires et Pirogues Construits par les Habitants de l'Amé-rique. *It is a magnificent book and a very rare one, so his plans have been printed here in sizes that may seem rather lavish, but they are only slightly larger than the originals. Admiral Paris's pages tend to be confusing because many vessels are often worked in together at different scales. In order to show the large double canoes at their best, many of the smaller outriggers have been eliminated from the original plates.*

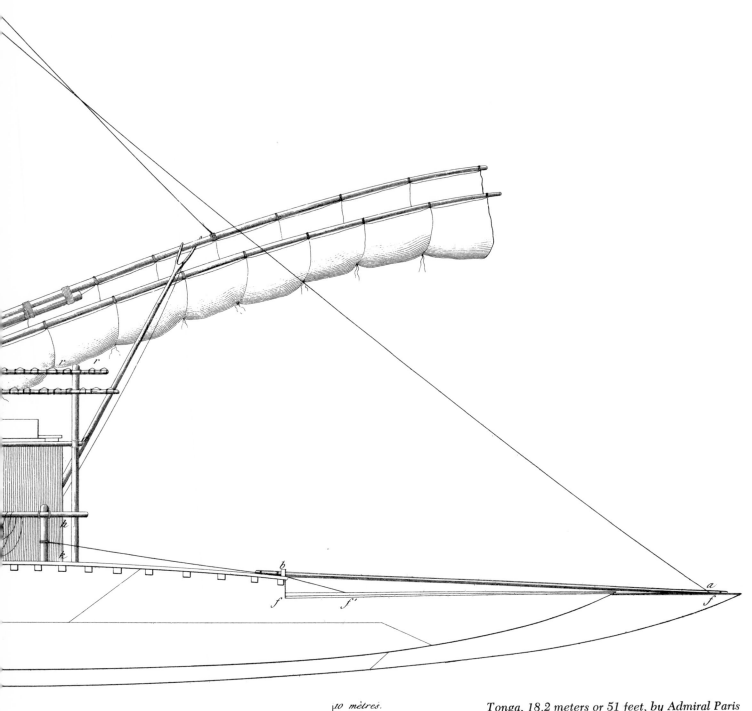

10 mètres.

Tonga, 18.2 meters or 51 feet, by Admiral Paris

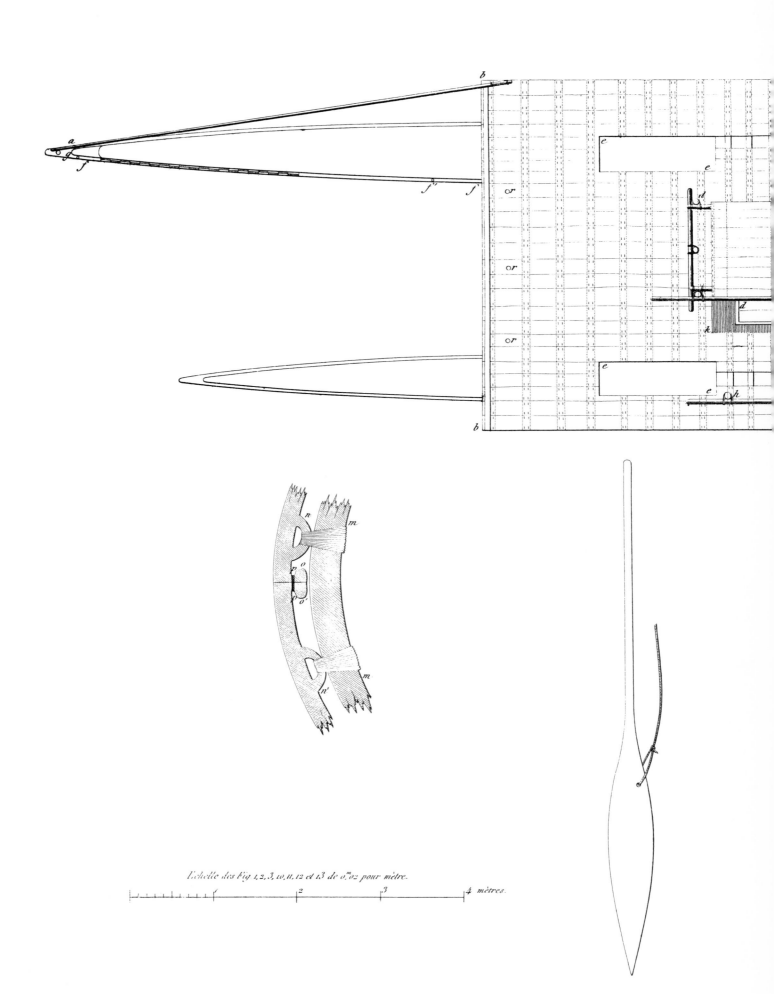

Échelle des Fig. 1, 2, 3, 10, 11, 12 et 13 de 0.ᵐ02 pour mètre.

2   3   4 mètres.

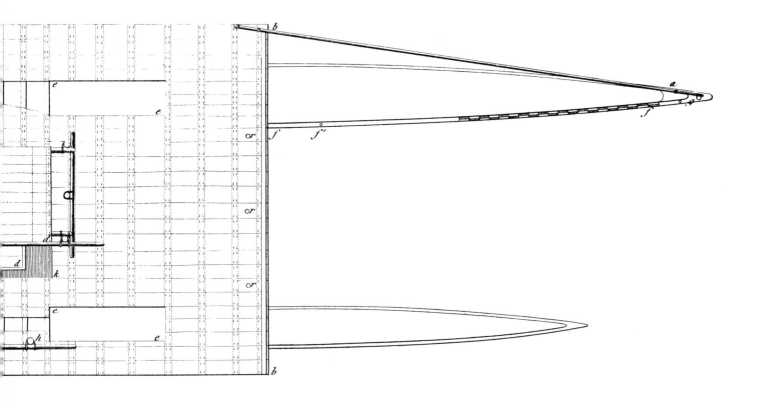

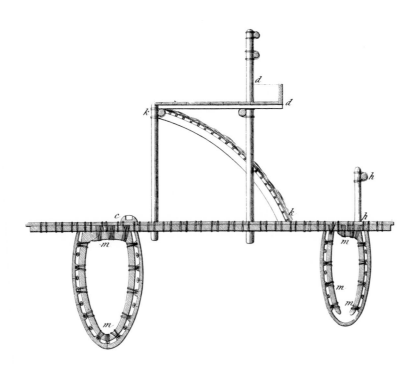

Echelle des Fig. 4, 5, 6, 7, 8 et 9 de 0.″01 pour mètre.

10 mètres.

Plan of the tongiaki *on preceding pages*

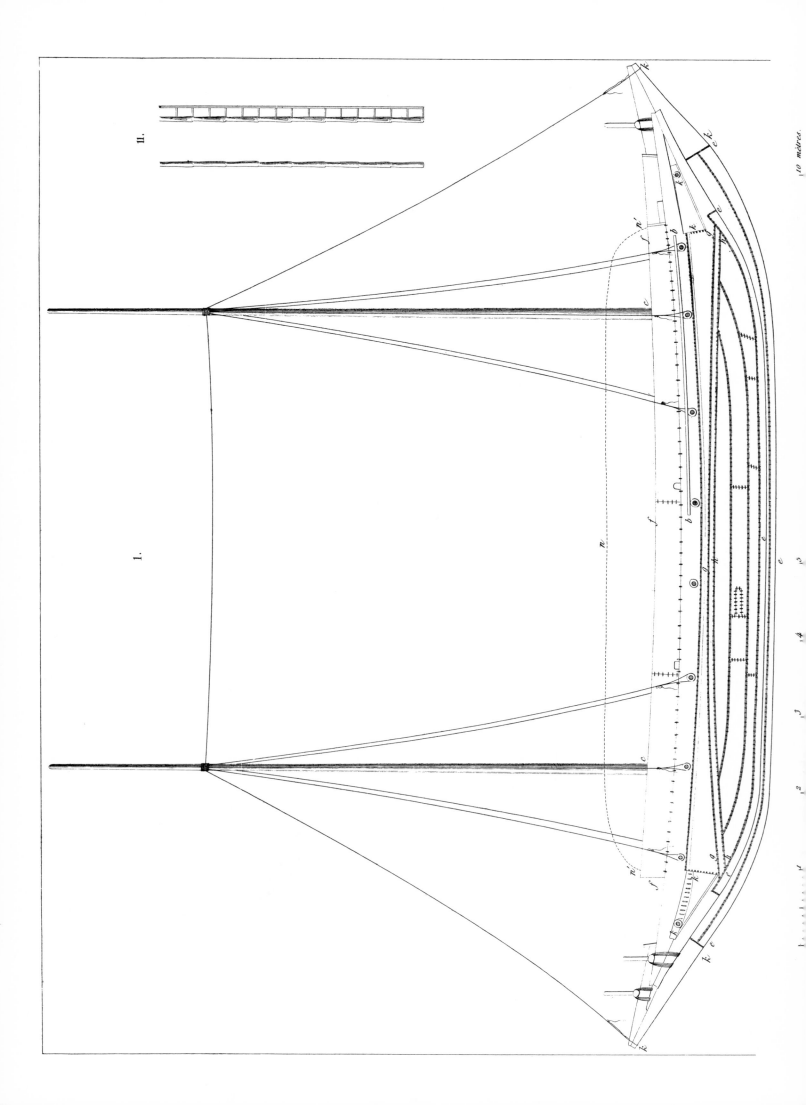

II.

I.

10 mètres.

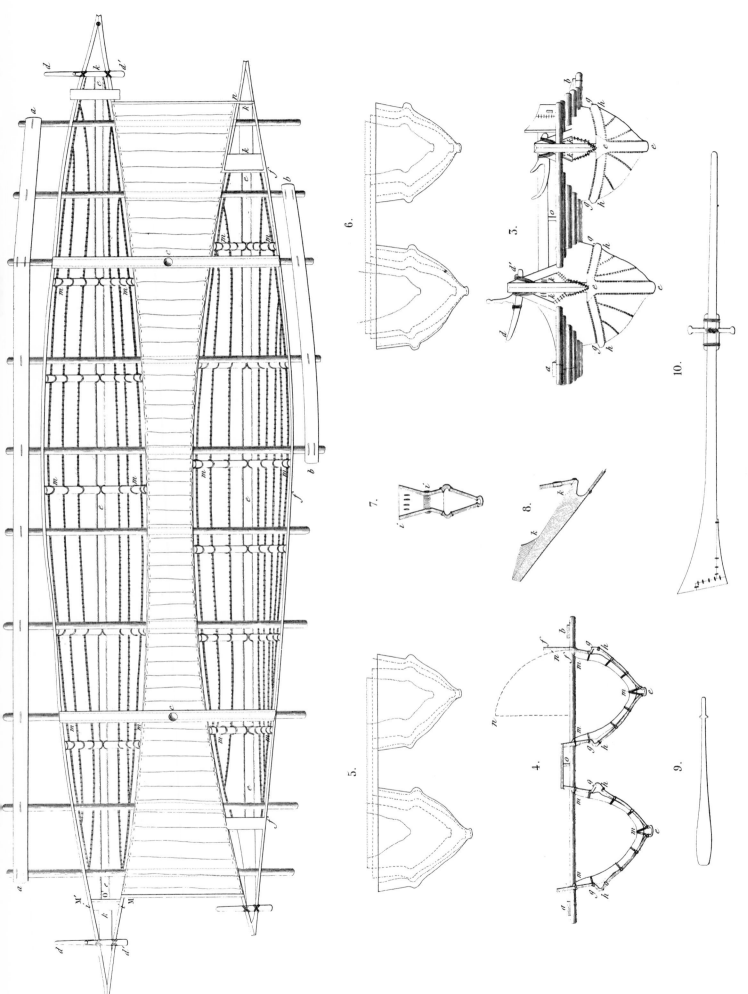

Tuamotu, 13 meters or 42½ feet, by Admiral Paris

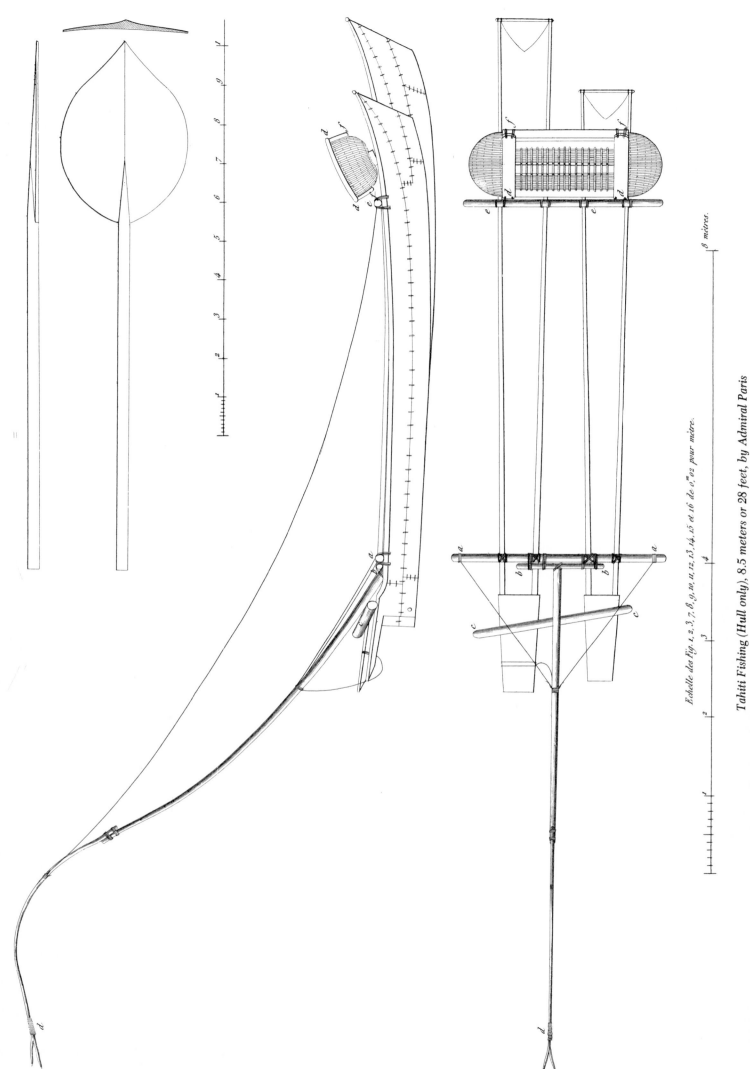

Echelle des Fig. 1, 2, 3, 7, 8, 9, 10, 11, 12, 13, 14, 15 et 16 de 0.m02 pour mètre.

8 mètres.

Tahiti Fishing (Hull only), 8.5 meters or 28 feet, by Admiral Paris

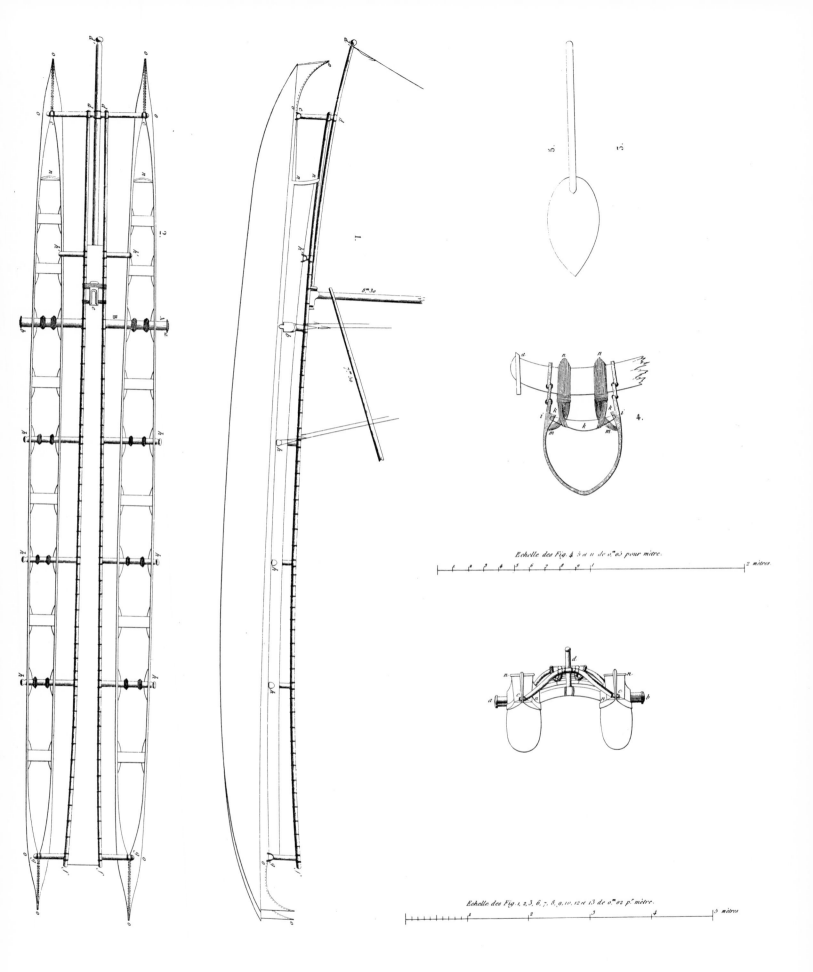

Hawaii, 16 meters or 52 feet, by Admiral Paris

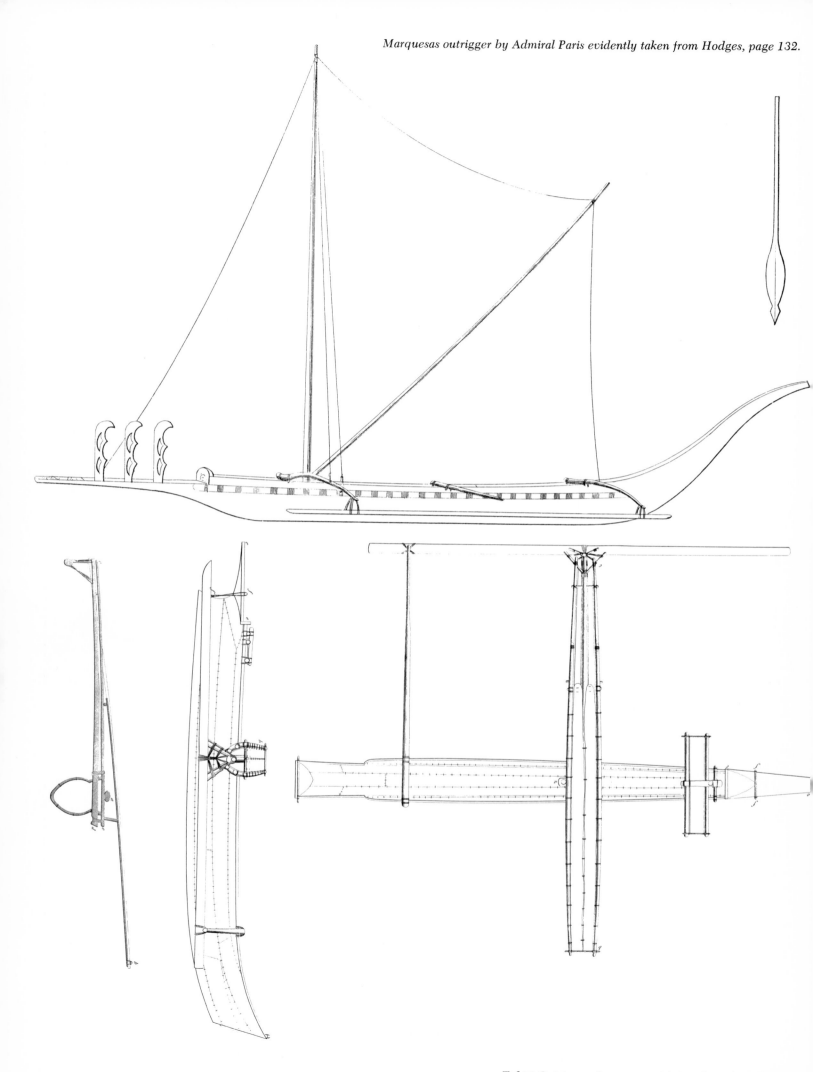

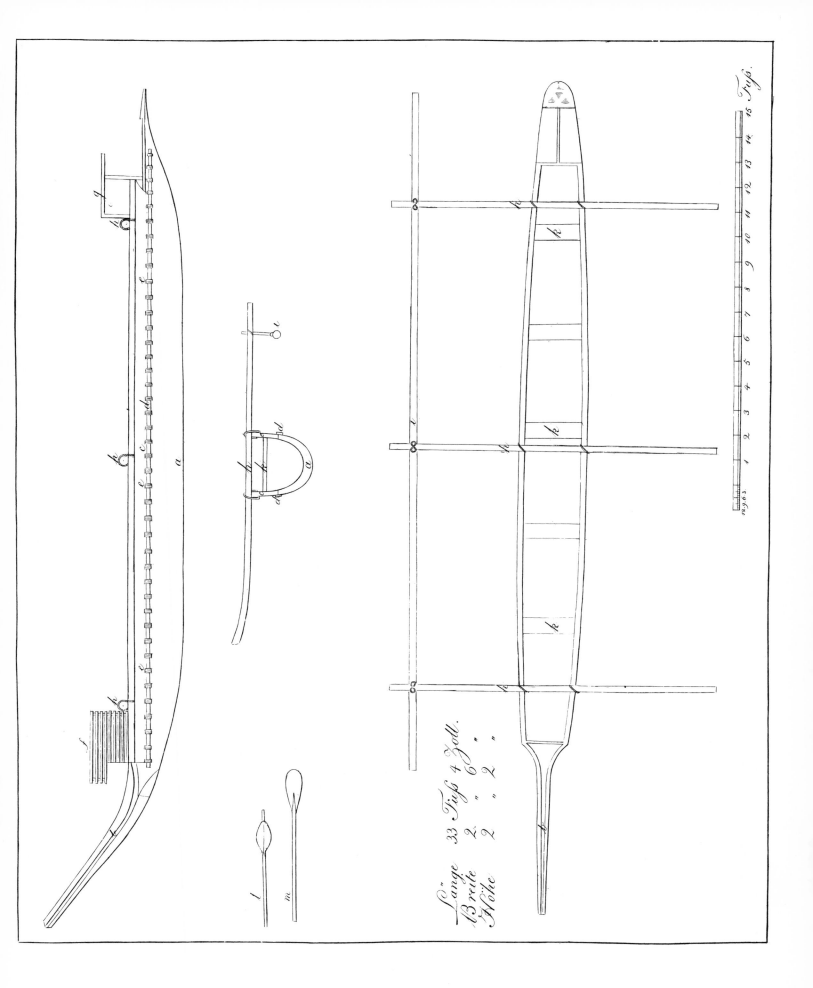

G. H. von Langsdorff accompanied Admiral von Krusenstern, the first Russian circumnavigator, 1803-1807, and published a splendid collection of plates, over 40 of them in
his account of the voyage of the frigate Thetis. His drawing of a Marquesan outrigger
canoe, page 133, leaves much to be desired, but this plan of one seems careful and accurate. The canoe is 33 feet.

PROVISIONING

Foodstuffs and Liquids

The provisioning of a canoe or a fleet of canoes was a most important undertaking, but it was not particularly difficult nor did it demand any special skills or imagination. Variety of cuisine has never been of much consequence to the Polynesian. It was not then and it is not today. Quantity is his chief concern; and cleanliness. Not that he is indiscriminate. You will find no man throughout the tropics who is more particular about eating a certain species of mango at the very moment it is at its best point of ripeness, and he knows his bananas with a subtlety of distinction between varieties and uses that temperate zone people never knew existed. He will rummage among a netload of fish and pick and choose like a Parisian housewife selecting cheeses fresh from the country.

But by and large his diet is bland and simple. Two animal meats were all he raised; pig and dog. The latter has been abandoned out of sympathy for the white man's horrors, but in the old days the little Polynesian dog, a very distinctive breed with hardly any variation throughout its wide island range, was considered the prime delicacy. All dogs were vegetarian, as carefully raised for their purpose as are our lambs, and never treated as pets. They existed only as foodstuff for man and were transported by him to many of the island groups but by no means to all. Or if they were introduced in some islands, they subsequently died out or were exterminated. The pig was more ubiquitous, but there are important islands where it, too, never survived or perhaps never arrived. Rats were omnipresent and the variety was edible, but they seem to have been a desperation diet rather than a gourmet one. The only universal warm-blooded meat was chicken; the small, scrawny, southeast Asian black cock that still pokes about the underbrush today. He is an independent creature who cannot be penned up yet never goes wild; a hardy little fellow whose hen's eggs are hidden in the twisting roots of a purau tree or in the recesses of a gardenia bush, always in a secret nook known only to the children, and whose crow persists through all the small hours of the night.

All three of these would have been taken live in the voyaging canoe, some for eating on the way, some for breeding at the new settlement. As far as we know, their flesh was seldom cured in salted, smoked, dried, or other fashion. The Maori used to store cooked pigeons in their own fat. Teuira Henry says that Tahitians were "expert at killing birds with which the hills abound," so perhaps they, too, potted the flesh, but if so, no trace of such a practice has remained.

The preserved foods were vegetable. The chief staple and by far the longest lasting was *mahi* or fermented breadfruit. In the Marquesas *ma* or *popoi-ma* was said to be best when ten years old, *ma-tahito;* and in 1920 Handy saw some that was a hundred years old at Tahuata. In the Tuamotus, Emory found long-lasting pandanus flour still in use in the early 1900s. But there were many others; so many plants and with so many varieties that it may be interesting to take a list, of eatables only, from Teuira Henry.

TAHITIAN NAME	KIND OF VEGETABLE	NUMBER OF VARIETIES
uru	breadfruit	±40
teve	small tuber	?
meia	banana	34
fei	mountain banana or plantain	18
taro	large tuber	29
ti	root	13
ape	arum	?
umara	sweet potato	6
uhi	yam	2+
to	sugar cane	10
niu or haari	coconut	16
mape	chestnut	3
ahia	mountain apple	?
fara	pandanus	19
ieie	buds of the vine	?
tou	nut	?
autoraa	almond	?
huehue	gourd	?

And let Captain Wilson add a couple.

"Yappe. A mountain root, larger than the tarro. It requires to be well dreffed, as the raw juice is acrid, and fets the tongue and lips in a great heat, but when properly prepared is very good food."

"E'vee, improperly called the yellow apple, is as large as a nonpareil, and of a bright golden hue; but oblong, and different in fmell and tafte from our apples, more refembling a peach in flavour, as well as in being a ftone fruit."

. . . and comment on an important one that is less well known than it deserves. "Tee. A root of no great fize, growing in the mountains, fweetifh, and producing a juice like molaffes: when in want of other provifions, they dig it up and bake it. The leaves are used to line the pits for the mahie; and to thatch the temporary huts, in their excurfions to the higher regions. They make ufe of thefe alfo to fpare better clothes: with one of thefe leaves round their waifts as a maro, and the plantain over their fhoulders, they drefs for fifhing, or any dirty work."

Most of these would have been pounded to a paste, mixed with coconut cream wrapped in neat little leaf packages and cooked in the earth oven; when so

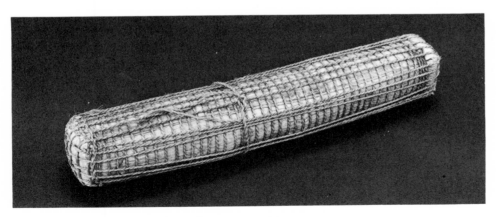

Pandanus flour prepared for a sea voyage

treated all would have tasted, to our palates, very much the same, but the slight variations would have been easily perceptible to the Polynesian and much relished.

There was, and is, a common confection made of sliced banana pulp, dried in the sun to a consistency of thick gum, wrapped in leaves and bound in fibers. It is an incredibly delicious sweetmeat that will last indefinitely and it must be highly nutritious.

Of course all of these vegetables would be carried also in the raw, mostly for replanting, but some also, especially bananas and sugar cane, for eating fresh as they went along. And in addition there would probably be nearly as varied and multitudinous an assembly of *tiare* slips, gourd seeds, bamboo shoots, *ava* roots for ceremony, *aute* twigs for bark cloth, *tamanu* nuts for the temple, and a host of other ferns, shrubs, trees. The habit must be long ingrained, for you rarely see a passenger on an inter-island boat today without a bundle of green sprouts for her relatives.

It is interesting to note that almost all of these fruits and vegetables destined for propagation were in root or shoot form. The Polynesian, like his distant ancestors in southeast Asia, did not deal with seed except in a few obvious cases. One of these was the utilitarian gourd; another was the most important of all of his foodstuffs; the coconut.

This leads us naturally to drinks, for the coconut was used as much for its "milk" as for its "meat." At the last minute of loading, coconuts must have been handed aboard to fill every cranny of every bilge until the gunwales were low. Fresh water was, however, the chief liquid cargo, stored in large bamboo joints and in gourds. Such containers would be lighter than our barrels or bottles and would keep the water sweeter.

A seeming digression

To cultural anthropologists like Vayda and others collected in his symposium, the accidental theory is appealing because from their point of view settlements seem to have been few and in rather small numbers of people. This harks back to the early assumption that if deliberate navigation was possible migration would have been massive. But here again is European thinking: there seems no good Polynesian reason to assume this. On the contrary deliberately navigated voyages would more likely have been single expeditions at lengthy intervals. Not many chiefs were adventurous or prosperous enough, nor moved by reasons compelling enough to undertake exploratory and settlement voyages. Not many navigators were masters of the art. The number of people transported must have been relatively small even if two or three canoes travelled together, considering all the freight that was necessary for settlement. Few if any of those on the initial expedition would have reasons or compulsions to go back. At home it was rarely or ever certain that the expedition had been successful.

Just because there was probably not constant or large scale movement does not at all mean that what long voyages did take place were all accidental. Apropos of provisioning in particular the evidence might be said to be mostly the other way. To account for the presence of "provisions" in accidentally settled lands, Sharp even goes to the absurd length of suggesting that pigs, dogs, and chickens may have drifted off all by themselves in canoes that broke away from their moorings in a storm. Who fed and watered them en route? Can you conceive that offshore fishermen, unexpectedly caught in a gale of wind, would happen to have banana sprouts, breadfruit shoots, taro roots, kava plants, paper mulberry, ti, all stowed away with pigs, dogs, chickens and womenfolk in the recesses of their bilges, sharing by chance the room that was intended for their catch of fish? Let us get on with more likely things.

A vital alimentary element was of course fish, the largest source, then and now, of protein. Fish were dried, salted or otherwise preserved for the voyage and dried octopus may also have been used, as it is today. Live fish were taken in bamboo baskets tied alongside, but these are clumsy contraptions for a long voyage and were probably used only for inter-island trips or for a first few days' supply. Naturally fishing at sea was constant, but probably not very productive at any considerable distance from shore. Indeed to the modern ichthyologist the central Pacific is a vast arid desert compared to the fertile expanses of the other oceans. Except, of course, that there are oases. Within a hundred miles or so of the island clusters, marine life teems. Another exception is the flying fish; they are multitudinous over the farthest deeps, and since they are so easy to catch low down on the surface, lured by a light at night, they must have been an important source of nourishment. Still another is the porpoise that occurs frequently on the open sea and is exceptionally good eating.

Another wild species that helped were sea birds, especially the boobies, so named unfortunately for their tameness. The most common birds were white terns, sooty terns, brown boobies, blue-faced boobies, red-tailed tropics, and frigates. But they never flew far from land. Still a very small, isolated island that would be of little apparent use to man was likely to support a prodigious population of birds feeding on the fish in its surrounding waters and nesting densely ashore. A brief stopover to collect eggs and fresh poultry would be well worth a few days' detour. Such islands are not common, but they do turn up, and in their waters there could also be found turtles, dolphins, and fish. The catching of a hefty tuna weighing a hundred pounds or so would make a big difference in the balance of the larder.

A fair amount of cooking was probably done at sea, especially during the first week or two. The double canoe carried a sandbox forward, and most likely a fire was kept going much of the time. They were not dependent on perpetual flame because they could always make fire by rubbing sticks, but this might have been more tedious at sea than nursing a small bed of coals. Pork would be cooked, of course, and dog, chicken, and fish; also fresh breadfruit and fei which would last a week or more from departure. But the mainstays, *poi* and *mahi*, having been precooked, would be eaten cold, and fish was frequently eaten raw, especially for its juices if water was scarce.

How much could they carry? And how long would it keep them at sea? George Robertson, who was Captain Wallis's master on the *Dolphin*, wrote in 1767 at Tahiti, ". . . here we saw two very large double Canoes about fifty feet Long, which I dare say would have carried near Eight tun . . ." Captain Wilson of the *Duff* writes of double canoes 60 to 90 feet long with sixty to a hundred paddlers, capable of carrying three hundred men. Three hundred men at 160 pounds each would denote a capacity of 48,000 pounds. Robertson's more modest vessels would carry 8 "tun," or 17,600 pounds.

If, for an exploratory voyage, we hypothesize a 50-foot double canoe carrying twenty-four men (two relays of ten paddlers each, two steersmen, a *tahuna* and a chief) at an average of 160 pounds per man, we arrive at about 4000 pounds of *homo sapiens* leaving 13,600 pounds for gear and provisions. At 6 pounds per day per man (3 pounds of food and 3 pounds of water) we could calculate a consumption rate of 144 pounds a day. This amount, predicated on a 32 day voyage, leaves a surplus carrying capacity for double the rations estimated above with plenty of allowance for gear as well. Twenty-four men seems about as many as could be crowded into a fifty foot vessel, but Cook had about 85 in a ship only twice as large. Working explorers packed them in. On the whole it seems unlikely that their cruising ranges would be seriously cramped because of provisions, especially since rain water and fish have not been taken into account.

As for their stamina Ben Finney's new scientific tests may bring surprises, but remember that a man has recently rowed single-handed across the Atlantic.

And so with a good store of staples, fresh and cooked, with a few live animals and an occasional catch of fish, with a random rain squall to replenish the water supply and a providential atoll to fortify the protein supply, the Polynesian, taking advantage with uncanny knowledge and skill of every edible morsel in his path, was not likely to fare too badly in his own particular ocean area.

Farewell

After the canoe had been launched, it might have been weeks or months, possibly even years, before the grand departure took place. Certainly the season would have to be the right one for the star path to be followed. In any sidereal year a long-distance voyage could set out only during one particular moon or perhaps some phases of moons preceding or following it. This was the single, fixed annual factor; no voyage could be commenced until the stars were right; all other elements had either to anticipate or wait for that. Since the building of a canoe would take many months, perhaps a year, with many unpredictables that might delay completion, it seems unlikely that a chief with an urge to migrate could deliberately plan in advance for any one chosen season. Precise planning is not in the nature of a Polynesian. More likely he would commence the realizing of his vision in only loosely related stages, choosing the trees, cutting and shaping, refinement in the shed by the waterside and then the final assembly, the launching and rigging followed by the testing and selecting and training of a crew. After all this, the craft might well be taken to pieces and redistributed in the community, to await the mood of the chief or the prophecies of the *tahuna* or a sign from the gods.

When the portents began to loom favorably, there would then come a period of intense preparation: reassembling the canoe, preparing the provisions and, most important, preparing the spirits of the voyagers for the long venture ahead. The whole community was deeply and intricately involved.

In this final stage the specific star season must have been fairly accurately anticipated, but probably only in a vague way, well ahead of time because there might easily be a period of waiting of several weeks or months before the master starsman could give the final signal. And no one else, only he alone, would have been able to predict that time. Moreover, his predictions would always have been shrouded in mysteries that could never, for them, be timed, as for us, by calendars and clocks. Actually they were timed, and to a nicety, except that their calendars and clocks were not the common tools of all men but the exclusive arcana of the few priestly *tahuna*.

But at last to a common seaman would come the long-awaited, pre-selected day. He would never know, nor even want to know why or how that particular day was chosen, but he would never question its rightness; to him it would have come strictly from the gods by way of the curling perhaps of the intestines of a sacrificial pig.

And so with a faith secure in his heart and a thrill of purpose in his blood, he would say a last, lingering farewell to his shore-bound loves and wade out into the lagoon to leap aboard the great double-hulled vessel, to hand in the last few coconuts, to take up his paddle and at the final signal to strain with all his strength to propel the canoe with his fellows toward the pass that would let them out of the calm water and onto the ocean swells. Then up sail and out bailer. Let fly the long streaming pennants of tufted tapa. Cover over the hull openings especially in the bows with stout mats securely lashed to fend off the spray. Scramble aft to trim sail; agile activity all over the boat to set her on the right slant of wind, trimmed to the precise course as directed by the uplifted eyes and guiding hand of the master navigator.

When at last the ship was securely on her way, there was time to sit back and take a last look astern at the home island fading perhaps forever into the twilight.

160

NORTH/SOUTH VOYAGING

Hawaii First

We should remember that almost all of the speculation and study that has been done on Polynesian navigation has come from either New Zealand or Hawaii. Even the most dispassionately scientific of these investigators seem to be influenced by their own north/south orientations. That is only natural and it would be strange if they were not. It would be foolish to imply that this makes them biased. It merely means that the migrations that settled their own lands are usually uppermost in their minds and that they then tend to resolve the whole problem as a whole. That was the way we resolved our problem of navigation; by developing and applying a theoretical scientific concept that was worldwide in scope. We must constantly remind ourselves that the Polynesian did nothing of this sort. He navigated as best he could in the circumstances where he found himself, and this led him into two distinct methods that were essentially different even though they had much in common.

Kjell Akerblom has pointed out most perceptively the differing systems in Micronesia, at least two of them, each suited to the particular conditions of their separate areas and both of them different from the Polynesian methods. It would not be pertinent to summarize them here because they are not systems devised for exploratory and migratory voyages, but rather for median-distance inter-island intercourse.

In Polynesia the first system was, of course, the fore-and-aft star path applicable only to east/west courses in equatorial latitudes. These were conceived and born in a reciprocal relationship between Samoa-Tonga-Fiji in the west and Tahiti-Tuamotu-Marquesas in the east. This migration, settlement, and intercourse took place over a period of possibly a thousand years; let us approximate from 500 B.C. to 500 A.D. During that time the great double canoes were perfected, and along with them offshore navigation or "pilotage" was expanded and refined. This might preferably be called *sensory* navigation, the use of the senses; of sight to interpret visual signals from clouds, lagoon reflections, volcanic smoke, swell patterns, seaweed, bird flight, and such like; the use of smell for land odors; of taste for offshore fish and alternations in salinity; of hearing for breakers and winds; of feeling for wave and swell motions, wind changes, temperature variants; in other words, a whole tapestry of sensory perception and response to the immediate environment and in the process an important storing of all that knowledge in the memory.

This could not have been gained without a previous mastery of celestial or what we might call *intellectual* (as contrasted to sensory) navigation. It was the fore-and-aft method with its adjuncts, such as the zenith star and three-stars-in-line, that first enabled the Polynesian to crisscross the huge ocean expanses and thus to extend his sensory method beyond the offshore or pilotage range. After many,

161

many centuries of blue-water sailing under the guidance of horizon stars, he would feel enough at home on the open sea within his massive rectangle so that he could begin to venture outside of it. And most importantly he would gradually come to know it so well that he could find himself pretty much anywhere within it. It would thus become a huge home base area that he could not miss on returning, as he progressively ventured outside it, even while he was learning that he could not rely on his fore-and-aft star path method when he was heading more north/south than east/west.

Once arrived at that state of grand familiarity with the area itself and once master of the sensory experience gained within it, it is not difficult to imagine him casting about for other means of guidance to other island clusters. The most obvious one that he could not have failed to notice was, of course, the migratory flights of birds. He had used birds for signals for a long time and he knew them well. But in his east/west traipsing, they were to him merely outlying indications of land, homing birds that plied their offshore courses; out in the morning to feed, back in the evening to roost. They kept at their eternal habits, conveniently for him, all the year round with never a variation from the established patterns.

But at certain seasons of the year, every year, other quite different species of birds drew his attention to other quite different habits. These flew in long-drawn-out flocks, not singly or in small groups as did his local island birds. And their rhythms were quite different, too. They would fly over in a skein that took several days or even weeks to pass and they always followed the same flyways. Coming out of the south, they headed north when the *matariki* rose for the new year on the horizon at sunset. Then, six months later, they returned from the pit of the Great Dipper toward the pit of the Southern Cross. Theirs clearly was a seasonal flight, quite different from the familiar diurnal one.

It did not take much detective ability to tell the Polynesian that these birds were flying from one group of islands to another. The golden plover, and the bristle-thighed curlew came south from Alaska by way of Hawaii to Tahiti in the winter, lived in the mountains for the season, departed north in the summer and returned again next year and every year . . . on the dot of the proper moon. They were small birds, many of them. He must have reasoned that they could not fly very much further than he could voyage in his canoe. There was bound to be land at the end of their journey, new land to him. So what was more logical than to take after them?

They had not come from any old place in the south, nor did they head in any old direction in the north. From the Tahiti-Nukuhiva complex they made an invariable course barely to the west of north, and in the other direction other birds, notably the bob-tailed godwit, the long-tailed cuckoo and the shining cuckoo made an equally unconfused course well to the west of south as they made their unerring way to New Zealand. These are the only bird migration paths in the central Pacific that are of notable consequence. There are a few east/west migrations, but since they began and ended within his own known rectangle or into enemy territory to the west, they would have little mystery or interest for him. The other two led to two places and those two only. He did not know them at first, but he found them out in time. In the north they were what he called Hawaii and in the south what we call New Zealand.

The significance of bird migration on Polynesian migration is a controverisal subject. The enthusiasts emphasize the reliability of the seasonal flights and the ease with which they could be followed from a canoe, their cries at night, etc. The skeptics point out that birds are not subject to currents or lateral drift, nor could their instinctively readjusted courses be followed after an offsetting storm. Andrew Sharp even produces a caustic illustration, a blank grey disc entitled ". . . The diagram represents prehistoric navigators looking for migratory birds at night."

It seems to me they both miss the point. Migratory birds were not navigational instruments, they were an indication, nay, they were a proof positive that land lay in the direction in which they flew. It was easy enough to determine that direction over a period of time and over a relatively short distance. Birds do not beat about a bush, especially at sea. They make direct course to their targets. This course can easily be determined and then fixed by star courses with their usual attendant aids, swells, winds, etc. So the Polynesian did not need to follow the birds from day to day. He did not need to see them or hear them at night. All he needed was to find the way in which they pointed and pursue it to its inevitable end.

He headed northerly first for a number of good reasons. Excursions to the south had taught him that he would soon encounter discouragingly cold weather and even many exploratory journeys uncovered no stepping-stone islands along the way. Moreover the winds were contrary and fickle, unlike his familiar trades, and the currents kept setting him severely off his course. To the north, on the contrary, the climate held his own good warmth as far as the equator and as far as the Hawaiian islands beyond it. There was an area of fitful winds and calms, but it was also an area of plentiful rains and of better fishing than he was accustomed to on his open sea. There were also a few islands along the way (Starbuck, Christmas, Palmyra), small, barren, and isolated but fine for birding, eggs, and fishing. It must have taken many shorter-range exploratory voyages out and back to discover them, but once located they greatly extended the scope of his quest. Most agreeable of all aspects of the northern passage were the steady, smiling beam winds from the east. Except in the doldrum area, they gave him the best of sailing both going out and coming back.

It was not long before he could see the pole star, and that was convenient, too. But it was not so important to him as most European Euclidean navigators have thought. He was accustomed to seeing the Cross revolving around the black pit of the south celestial pole. And he was also accustomed to watching the Great Dipper swing around an opposite pit that he could not see because it was below the horizon but that he must have realized was there. Those "poles" were useful to him to give him an idea of how far out he was or how far back he had to go to get them into his home-zone balance, but they did not give him precise latitude in our sense, so they were not crucial, but they kept him going steadily, north or south.

The whole of our navigational concept is dependent on precision and a very small deviation from precision thus naturally results in a large error and a fearful uncertainty. That is why perhaps so many experts consider Polaris so important. Polaris marks the celestial north pole with a most fortunate accuracy for our instruments. But if you are not an instrumentalist Polaris loses its magic and the black pit of the south celestial pole with its four great "pointers," Crux, the tail

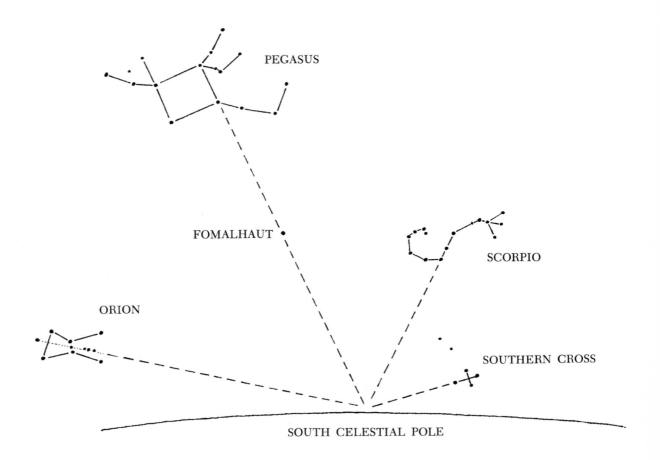

PEGASUS

FOMALHAUT

ORION

SCORPIO

SOUTHERN CROSS

SOUTH CELESTIAL POLE

of Scorpio, the chest of Pegasus aligned with Fomalhaut, and the head, mid-buckle and sword of Orion, are just as useful to give you what we would call a latitude but which would be to him a familiar bearing from the heavenly dome; one of many such bearings, not the all important single factor it is with us.

And in discrediting early or prehistoric navigators our astronomically sophisticated experts are quick to point out that 2000 or 3000 years ago Polaris did not coincide (as it almost exactly does today) with the celestial north pole. It was several degrees out. "And then where would they be?" This was no great trouble for them. An off center Polaris and the pointers of the Great Dipper were just as good guides to the old Polynesian as their southern counterparts.

These men were using areas, not precise points. Areas of sky told them where areas of land lay; screens of islands lying below screens of stars. Everything was of course approximate but they had accustomed themselves over long centuries of voyaging to deal comfortably with approximations and to use all of their senses in doing so.

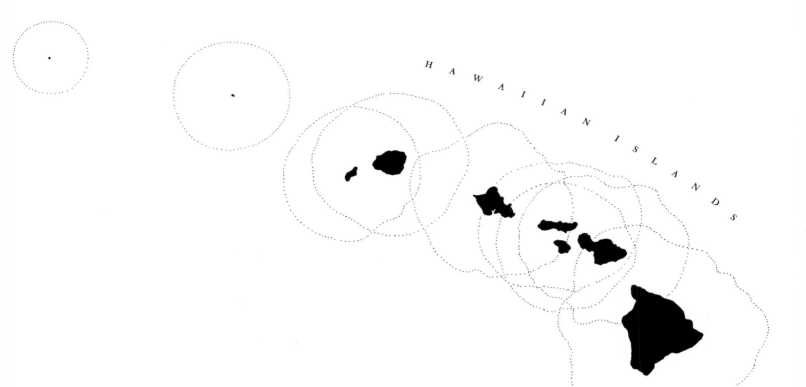

The Hawaiian Screen

But if Polaris was not crucial to them what did soon come to be so was a bright fire high in the night sky. Mauna Loa could probably be seen as much as 200-300 miles away if it was erupting as it probably was in those days more often than now. And it can be seen 90 miles away in daylight. Moreover, the Hawaiian chain of islands stretched about 400 miles across his course. They made a pretty target and it lay right in the path of those migrating birds . . . So Hawaii was first discovered and later settled about 500 A.D.

It would have been a long time before that canoe load or that "fleet" load could have built up into a new civilization in that new land. There would have been too much to do ashore; just keeping alive the five to seven years that must pass before the new coconuts ripened was enough to preempt the immediate building of a new canoe. Several generations at least, several hundred years perhaps would pass before they reached a stage of revived technology that would permit them to go back. And even then, why do it? The land was good here. Old enemies as well as old friends lay at home.

This may seem a rather cavalier account of navigation to Hawaii, taking much for granted. But the conditions prevailing for that voyage have been so well argued and so well demonstrated, especially of late by Ben Finney in his article "New Perspectives on Polynesian Voyaging" that there seems little point in repeating them in detail here. What they boil down to is this. If you first grant purposeful long-distance voyaging, and the postulated east/west migrations by fore-and-aft star paths ought to make this credible, then the trip to Hawaii was relatively easy. There were currents to set canoes laterally off course and there was always sailing leeway, but storms were a negligible factor and the target was so broad that errors in allowing for current and leeway offsets could be largely discounted in a run that was as short in time as this one.

Track of the American Barquentine Kate G. Pedersen
Sydney to San Francisco, 1924

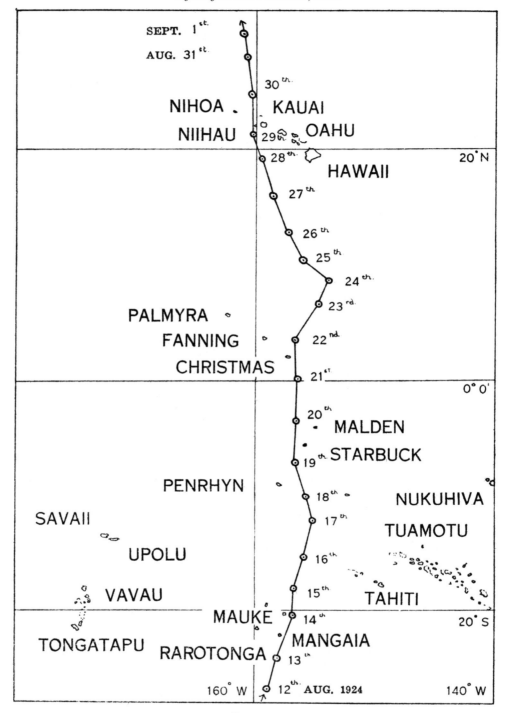

Comment

Throughout this 20-day run the ship was on the starboard tack, sailing full and by, about seven points from the wind. The course was the natural track of the ship between noon positions and included current and leeway.

166

The note in the log book indicates the steadiness of wind and weather; the ship was under full sail all the time. The only squalls were experienced on 24th August, and these were not sufficiently strong to necessitate reducing sail.

The average daily run was 177.5 miles and the average speed over the ground was 7.4 knots.

The track, laid off on a chart, shows that the traverse passed close eastward of Mangaia and Mauke, eastward of Penrhyn, westward of Starbuck and Malden, thence close to the east of Christmas Island, and on to Niihau. It is of interest to note that after 17 days of natural sailing by the wind, between Mangaia and Niihau, the westing made was less than 60 miles.

Sea conditions were good throughout, mostly a slight swell and moderate sea; no sea, or even spray, was shipped. Conditions were such that a well-found canoe could have made a similar passage.

—Primitive Navigation in the Pacific, *by Capt. G. H. Heyen, 1962*

*   *   *

Instinctively the experienced *tahuna* would allow for leeway by sailing closer to the wind than he would if he were heading directly for his target. It can also be assumed that any veteran navigator is aware that on the open ocean the surface current runs with the wind, so to counteract that he would head closer still. The easterly beam winds that prevail throughout this course except in the doldrum belt gave him plenty of room for manuever. The north star soon became a made-to-order, fixed guide that would always point him in the direction in which he wanted to go. He did not need to worry about a stern star; indeed, it would have been of no use to him on his great circle course, except when he was returning southward. He might allow too much compensation for current and leeway by pinching too much to the east. Or he might not allow enough by falling off too far to the west. But his target was so broad, 400 miles, that even if he consistently erred one way or another by half a knot he would find himself off center only 180 miles in fifteen days, easy enough to make up once he hit the Hawaiian chain.

Now this, of course, is assuming a return or second voyage after the islands had been discovered and he had learned how to trim his sails to the prevailing wind and adjust the direction of his canoe at right angles to the rising and the setting sun. The first voyage of discovery would have been largely luck based this time on his conviction that the golden plover knew that he was going toward land. But all first voyages had been luck. Fortunately the great arc of islands was there, and though it may have been luck that brought him to them the first time, we can be fairly certain that he had made many preliminary voyages, aligned with the fly-way of the birds, progressing gradually further and further north until that luck turned up on the horizon.

After that he relied on new skills to repeat it; skills that were different in a navigational sense from his east/west equatorial techniques. Fore and aft stars were now virtually abandoned. To be sure he would use Polaris ahead for his general northerly course and Polaris astern going back south. He would keep his course carefully at right angles to his familiar equatorial stars, both rising and setting, using them both to his right and to his left. At the same time he would be guided by the relatively constant winds and the even more constant, in fact almost invariable, east-west swell and, during the day, by the rising and setting of the sun. This was all equatorial sailing from the southern tropics to the northern tropics with Polaris always mounting to position his progress. On this run the whole celestial pattern becomes a sort of "latitudinal" tunnel supplemented by a "latitudinal" swell floor, making it easy to check a shift in the one possible variable, wind. We might invent a new name for it and call it the "beam-bearing" system. It was not nearly as precise as the fore-and-aft system, but precision was not important in gaining two such wide targets as Hawaii to the north and his homeland to the south. We can dismiss the possibility that he would slip unbeknownst between the islands of the Hawaiian archipelago, because he would have known well just how high Polaris stood in the heavens when he was in their neighborhood. Once arrived in that area, or latitude as we would call it, he would sail a zigzag course east or west until he found an island.

That there were a number of trips back and forth seems the only way to account for different cultural evidences at different periods. But these reciprocal trips were probably few, much fewer than if our European explorers had done the discovering.

The Legend of Tafai

The most reliable and prolific collector of Tahitian legends and lore was the Rev. J. M. Orsmond, who presented his life's work in manuscript to the French Government in 1848. Thirty years of painstaking research and recording had gone into it and almost immediately it disappeared forever in the Ministère des Colonies in Paris. Fortunately Mr. Orsmond had a bright and hard-working granddaughter named Teuira Henry, who set to work some forty years later on the voluminous notes and papers that were the basis of his original work and eventually her classic work on Polynesian culture, *Ancient Tahiti,* was published in 1928.

One of the last legends collected from Tamera, a priest, in 1855 and later supplemented by Peue of Fautau and Teiva Vahine of Tiarei recounts the adventures of a widely known traditional Tahitian hero, Tafai. It is long and rambling and repetitive, as are all good Polynesian legends, starting with a genealogy that is typical except that there is particular concern here with Tafai's famous grandmother Nona, who was a cannibal goddess with long sharp teeth. Most of Tafai's immediate family were tricked by her and devoured, but he turned the tables on her and escaped to perform great feats of his own. Here is a selection of his seafaring exploits as recounted in *Ancient Tahiti.*

*   *   *

"Tafai's first great deed for the good of his country was the cutting of the sinews of this fish, Tahiti, to render it stable, and after accomplishing this he said they must cut the sinews of all the islands around Tahiti, which were detached parts of the fish, and that they must also go on and draw up new land from the sea. So a great double canoe was built, which he named the Anuanua (Rainbow), and valiant navigators and a priest were chosen to accompany him. He himself was the pilot and astronomer. He took his *tao* (an ironwood shoulder spear 12 feet long and pointed on both ends), which no other man in Tahiti could lift, and his paddle, which no one else could wield; and he prepared a great long line of *roa,* attached to an immense wooden fishhook, which was filled with magic at his touch. His men prepared their fishhooks and lines, which he also enchanted, and after the usual religious ceremonies they set out to sea.

"They went northwest to little Tahiti (Moorea-the-offshoot), and they thrust their spears into its quivering sinews and made it stable; they went southwest to Mairo-iti (Little-claw), which had fallen away from Moorea, and soon made it stable. They went north of Tahiti and found the islets of Te-tiaroa (Standing afar-off) struggling to rise above the foaming sea. So they threw down their hooks and drew them up one by one. Then with their spears they cut the sinews and fixed the islets in their present positions. They went on eastward and found that Me-tu

169

(Standing-thing; in modern Tahitian, Metia) was already fixed in its place. Then Tafai said they must go to other regions and fish up land, and they came to the Tai-o-vaua (Shaven-sea) and there beneath the mighty breakers, found the extensive Tuamotuan group, which they fished up and which ever since has remained as beautiful atolls and islets fringed with beds of coral of all hues and with pearl oysters. To these he added the high Mangarevan group and other hilly islands eastward that were also struggling to rise.

"They went on exploring the trackless ocean northward and drawing up islands, which they discovered by observing the sea dancing over them, until at last they perceived a mighty commotion apart from all others, and on approaching it they found the Hawaiian group all huddled close together beneath the sea level. Tafai first drew up Ai-hi (Bit-in-fishing, now called Hawaii), whose high twin mountains rose from their watery bed and went on rising until they reached an amazing height and were lost among the clouds, and whose shores extended beyond the horizon. Owing to the great volcano perpetually burning, this island was afterward named Havaii in the south. Tafai next drew up Maui, which he named M-au-i after the hero, Ma-u-i of eight heads, who detached the sky from the earth. This island also rose to a wonderful height. So they went on until all the islands were drawn up, and then those intrepid navigators went south and returned with people to dwell on the beautiful new land, bringing with them their gods, their chiefs and bread-fruit and other plants.

"At length the emigrants of the north and their kindred in the south, regretted that they were so widely separated from each other, and Tafai, who had returned home, conceived a plan to remove the Hawaiian islands to the south. He and his seaman prepared strong ropes, and invoking the gods to their aid they attached each island to the canoe. When all was made ready, Tafai warned his people to be guarded against breaking the sacredness of the spell that was to pervade their great undertaking. No one must speak or look back when in motion, on pain of displeasing and losing the aid of the gods. The great canoe moved off drawing the ropes, united in one, each man plying his paddle and looking steadily ahead, when soon a magical spell caused the islands to yield and follow in a most orderly manner, and onward they went. Shouts of applause which the navigators were rejoiced to hear, arose from the land but they swerved not from their purpose and still kept silence. All nature chimed in rejoicing, and above the sound of the steady breeze and rippling sea arose the chorus of people and birds singing, cocks crowing, hens cackling, dogs barking and occasionally pigs grunting, while overhead the sea gulls screeched their contentment. Still the mariners did not look back, nor did they speak, and the islands moved on.

"But finally the sound of the *hura* (Hawaiian hula) drum and flute arose, accompanied with songs of rejoicing from the people, and this so stirred the hearts of the seamen that all except Tafai could no longer contain themselves, and with one common impulse they stood upon their seats and looking back began to dance and sing also, when suddenly the charm was broken, the ropes snapped, and they were forsaken by the gods! As a result of the impetus, before the islands became stationary, Havaiia went forwards and Kauai and Niihau backwards, the middle islands remained close together, and detachments from the island coasts formed islets. In vain did the seamen and people offer invocations and oblations to the gods to return, nor did the prayers of Tafai, who was blameless, prevail. So they were obliged to abandon the enterprise, and the Hawaiian islands have remained forever an isolated group, standing grandly away in the north.

"Some years had elapsed after the travels of Taifai when the fame reached Tahiti of Te-ura-i-te-rai (Redness-of-the-sky), a beautiful princess in south Havaiia, who was to be obtained as a wife only by some valiant hero, and Taifai's cousins, the five sons of Pu-aa-ri-i-tahi, decided to go as aspirants for her hand. So they prepared a double canoe for that purpose. Tafai told his mother that he wished to go also, and so she took a coconut blossom sheath and laid it upon the sea, and it developed into a beautiful single canoe, which they named Niu (Coconut) and which was soon made ready for the voyage. His mother told him that his ancestral shark, Tere-mahia-ma-hiva (Speedy-travelling-with-fleet), would accompany him, and that he should address it as his guardian ancestor, which he agreed to do.

"The two canoes set out together. The double one was well manned with seamen, a pilot, and an astronomer; the single one had Tafai alone, escorted by the faithful shark, and it soon went far ahead of the other. Finally when the five brothers approached the shores of Havaiia, they saw awaiting them their cousin Tafai, who was the first to greet them on landing. The royal family of South Havaiia was soon apprised of the arrival of the young chiefs who had come to offer themselves to the princess, and they were well received by them. In the course of a few days the prowess of the young Tahitians was put to the test, and the beautiful young Hawaiian princess was herself chosen to be umpire for them. They were all girded and armed with spears for the encounter. First they were told to pull up by the roots an ava tree which was possessed by a demon, and which had caused the death of all who had attempted to disturb it. Each man was to come forward according to his age. Beginning with the eldest, Te-ura-i-te-rai said:

"'E Arihi-nui-apua o Tahiti e, a tii mai oe a iriti i te ava nei, e mama? e inu faataero i Havaii nei' (O arihi-nui-apua of Tahiti, come and pull up this ava, and chew it to drink and intoxicate Havaii).

"He went forward and thrust his spear in the stump of the tree, which like a living thing immediately darted forth its roots and pierced and killed him. Then came forward the second brother, Ta-oe-a-pua, who met with the same fate, and so it was with the three older brothers, Orooro-i-pua, Te-mata-tauia-ia-roo, and Te-mata-a-a-rai. Seeing that they were all dead, the princess said to their parents:

"'A tira paha' (That will do perhaps). But they replied that the last man must try. Then it was Tafai's turn and the princess said:

"E Tafai e, tari, Tafai-iri-ura, te turunu i Hawaii fanau Hema tau oroha! A tu mai oe a iriti i te ava nei, e mama, e inu e faataero i Hawaii' (O Tafai, pause! Tafai with red skin, who raised up Hawaii, born to Hema, my sympathies! Come and pull up this ava, and chew it to drink and intoxicate Hawaii).

"The noble red giant advanced undaunted and thrust his spear at arm's length into the stump of the ava. As the roots moved forwards to pierce him, he held tight the end of the spear, and they twisted around it like the arms of a devilfish, while he pushed the spear farther and farther into the taproot until the whole plant yielded. He drew it out, raised it still attached to the spear, beat and bruised the roots until they became powerless, and laid it down. Then he turned to his cousins lying lifeless upon the ground, and to the amazement of all the spectators he restored them to life.

"Soon the Tahitians were ready to make the drink from the ava roots, and as it was customary to have a feast on such an occasion they asked for a pig and necessary accompaniments. To this the royal family willingly agreed, and the pig they were to have was the renowned Moiri* (Whole swallower), a monster that swallowed live things whole and whose fame had long ago reached Tahiti. The slaying of this scourge to humanity was to be the last test of dexterity to which the young men were to be put; and they were to advance again according to their ages. So the young men, girded for the encounter, stood with their spears, and with sennit in their hands to tie the pig. The princess called out:

"'*E Moiri puaa e e fero mai!*' (O Moiri, be sennit bound!) Then rushing out of the woods, amid a cloud of dust which flew up under its heavy tread, came the terrible snorting and grunting monster.

"As the first champion dashed forward to catch the feet and throw the pig down he was swallowed whole, and one after the other of his brothers shared the same fate, their spears making no impression upon the thick hide of the animal. But as Tafai advanced, he thrust his spear down into the throat of the pig as it opened its great jaws to swallow him. The pig was slain, and immediately Tafai caused it to render up his five cousins, whom he once more restored to life. A great shout of applause rent the air, and Tafai was unanimously acknowledged to be the greatest hero that Havaiia had ever seen. The pig was the principal feature of the great feast that followed, and all ate of it. The ava that the Tahitians made was pronounced excellent and it rejoiced the hearts of the drinkers.

"Finally the time came for the hero of the day to claim his bride. The king and queen looked expectantly at Tafai and the princess, who had conceived great admiration for him and was willing to give him her hand. But what was their surprise when in the name of himself and his cousins he bade them all farewell, saying:

"'*Ia ora na ra outou, Te hoi nei matou i to matou fenua*' (Now fare you well. We are returning to our own land). Then the Hawaiians perceived that they had offended the Tahitians by their rigid treatment, and they could not prevail upon their visitors to change their purpose. Soon the Tahitians departed in the same way that they had come.

"When they returned home after their fruitless errand the Tahitians no longer aspired to seeking famed beauties of other lands, but took suitable wives from among their own countrywomen. Tafai married a fine young chiefess of North Tahiti, named Hina (Gray), famed for her beautiful raven hair, which when let loose, flowed down in waves to her feet and covered her graceful, majestic form; and their attachment for each other was strong and lasting.

"Tafai was prompt to go wherever duty called him in his own land and also in other lands and, as old records everywhere show, was beloved for his goodness and kind, generous deeds....

"It is not recorded in Tahiti that Tafai ever again went away from his native land, but it is stated that he and his wife lived long and happy together and that

---

*The pig, Moiri, may have been the fabulous monster, Kama-puaa (Child-pig) of the Hawaiians, which could change himself into a man or pig at pleasure. He was the husband of the fire goddess, Pele.

of them was born a son whom they named Vahi-e-roa* (Place-entirely-strange),

"In the manuscript dictionary by Mr. Orsmond, under the heading of the name Tafai are found these words: '*E atua Tafai-iri-ura, te turunu i Havai i. E mea navenave te aai o Tafai* (A god was Tafai of red skin, who raised up Havaii. Charming is the legend of Tafai).' In Tahiti his memory is perpetuated in the form of the beautiful club moss (Licopodium clavatum), named *rimarima Tafai* (fingers of Tafai), which is said to have sprung from his fingers after he left his earthly body and which grows prolifically among the ferns over all the islands; the spores of the plant are called *Maiuu Tafai* (fingernails of Tafai) which they are said to resemble."

*Vahi-e-roa figures in the legend of Rata, grandson of Tafai.

Maoriland Last

The discovery and settlement of New Zealand could have been inspired originally in much the same general manner as Hawaii. The long-tailed cuckoo was an even better trailblazer than the golden plover because he was more numerous, he flew lower down, and he made convenient noises in the night. There were also the bar tailed godwit and the shining cuckoo. The huge land mass was, in its way, an even better target than Mauna Loa. But the sea road was much more difficult and it was probably for that reason that the settlement came half a millennium later. A fore-and-aft star course could not be used because of great circle complications and a beam-bearing one would have worked only if

RAROTONGA

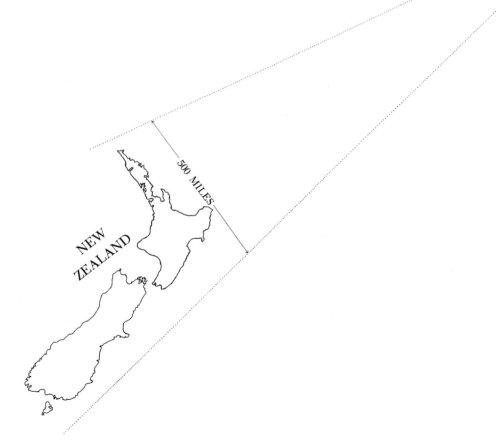

they had conceived of our old-fashioned and time-honored method of running down your latitude; that is sailing due south until they were in the latitudes of New Zealand, then sailing west until they hit the land. It seems to me quite conceivable that such experienced seamen could have divined this essentially simple method. From bird migration they knew where the land lay. The only chance they would be taking was its size and that turned out to be bountiful beyond all dreams. But by this time they were accustomed to generous archipelagos. However, it seems wisest, in deference to former arguments against Polynesian geometry, not even to suggest that latitude sailing was actually used.

In attempting the southern passage to New Zealand, the Polynesian would soon have run out of his familiar regular trade winds and there would have been no way to predict winds except by repeated exploratory voyaging. This he undoubtedly did; it was deep in his nature. And evidently several of them hit the mark for Aotea was peopled at several different intervals. He had one advantage over other long distance voyagers; whereas it is some 2200 miles from Tahiti to Hawaii, it is 1400 from Rarotonga to Whangarei.

New Zealand makes a poor argument for the accidentalists because it would be a strangely abnormal set of meteorological conditions that would ever blow anyone there from central Polynesia. Its geography practically demands deliberate settlement.

Down here we find a sort of myth, quite different from those of central Polynesia and Hawaii. This one is so specific and is repeated so often that it is tempting to accept it more literally. Kupe the wandering explorer, who is sometimes a demigod but more often a very human hero, came in his journeys upon the vast land of the long, white, cloud, *Aotea-roa*, and then returned to tell his people and to inspire them to follow his trail, steering always by the sun.

As Captain Hilder scornfully points out there are at least three versions of Kupe's legendary instructions. As he reduces them they are; "(a) Steer to the right of the setting sun, moon or Venus on the Orongonui (28th) of Tatau-uruora (November); (b) Steer to the left of the setting sun; and (c) Steer towards the rising sun." But to most people familar with myth and legend they are impressive simply because of their specificity, something rare in myths which were of course passed along from one story teller to another. A story teller who would disclose the details of such ancient legends to a white missionary or official would more likely deliberately mislead in revealing such secrets . . . if he knew them. More likely they were the arcane property of the priestly navigators alone who would never reveal them.

G. M. Dening, another distinguished contributor to *Polynesian Navigation*, points out two factors unusual in New Zealand waters that were peculiarly useful to the early navigator, a dependable and easily followed line of seaweed stretching to the eastward and the progression of changing currents and temperatures. Of course these are of use only when you know them well and would therefore apply only to gradually repeated voyages leading to discovery or to subsequent two-way voyaging.

How much two-way voyaging took place between these outlying provinces of Polynesia and the central homelands is a fiercely disputed naumachia. There is plenty of mythological evidence. The traditions abound with voyages setting forth. The expeditions of the heroes are so elaborately detailed in respect to building the canoes, selecting the seamen, provisioning, ceremony, and such like, that they read almost like historical records. Unfortunately for the literal-minded scholar, most of the heroes soon run into fabulous giant eels, miraculous sharks or yawning whirlpools, all of which converse like supernatural beings with them. Sometimes a canoe will even take to the sky and land its chief on a distant mountaintop. So these legends are dismissed by the skeptics with scorn. Perhaps they should be taken with many a grain of salt, but there should not be scorn. Too many of them have been recounted with too much wisdom and detail and faith for the whole body of them to be fictitious. Vague and ephemeral they may be, but surely they are echoes of a genuine widespread, long-lived, historical seafaring activity.

*   *   *

"It is now a recognized principle of philosophy, that no religious belief, however crude, nor any historical tradition, however absurd, can be held by the majority of a people for any considerable time as true, without having in the beginning some foundation in fact. . . . We may be sure that there never was a myth without a meaning . . . that there is not one which was not founded in fact, which did not hold a significance."—H. H. Bancoft, 1860

*   *   *

The great canoes have rotted away and the great navigating *tahuna* have long since died. Still the skeptics insist upon tangible evidence and there is no longer any to be found. They feel there must be remnants to verify their existence because they assume instinctively that the Polynesian, once his discovery was made, would ply his vessels back and forth in ever-increasing numbers as we have always done. They will agree comfortably with Alan Villiers when he says condescendingly, "But handsome and worthy as these double canoes were, they were not ships. They could not carry a regular and economical commerce over the seas." Commerce is his final yardstick and he is right. But the Polynesian never needed to be a trader and he never wanted to be. To be sure he did do a bit of inter-island exchanging of adzes for foodstuffs or mats, but his deep-sea voyaging was for exploration and settlement. Once settled, he might want to make a return voyage or two for additional transplants and to bring back news of his discovery, but after that the chances are he stayed put. Without trade there was little motivation for constant long-distance intercourse.

So his voyages were few, more like adventures than enterprises, more like ceremonies such as bringing the high chiefs of Aotea for investiture to the marae of Taputapuatea on Hawaiki (which is now called Raiatea), or more like abductions of princesses, or like banishments, or like flights from a diabolical chief.

So his ships were not ships. Too bad. But they did carry a cargo of culture over periods of many hundreds of years; a fairly good culture, too... and quite a distance it went. Once the great canoes had departed, there would not have been much incentive back home to send out another expedition. The last one may have been lost as far as they knew. Population pressures were relieved for a while.

Then one day in another generation or so some young dreamer in Tahaa or Hivaoa, in Mangareva or Manihiki, would start wondering about those old myths. He might take to watching the migrating birds on a spring evening. After a while he might go up in the mountains to search out a tree... suitable someday perhaps for a sea-going canoe.

Acknowledgments

I am indebted to many people for information and help. They are listed in the Bibliography usually with comments. In addition I want particularly to acknowledge the assistance of the staff of the manuscript room of the British Museum where so much of the original Cook material was made available to me: to the Mitchell Library in Sydney where Miss Suzanne Mourot, assistant librarian, did painstaking research and turned up material that I had not known existed: and as always to Margaret Titcomb and Judith Reed at the library of the Bishop Museum for all sorts of help. Helen Winfield has presided over an intricate production with a kindly, accurate, professional eye. Anne Kantor is due a bow for her help in design and in checking layout. Halliday Lithograph Corporation has performed exceptional photographic feats in extracting many clean drawings and plans directly from musty old books.

The artists who drew the illustrations are named in the captions throughout the book, but since these occur sometimes in groups each artist will be listed individually here. In addition the museum or collection to which I am indebted either for photography or for permission to use them will be indicated in italics. Since they are many and their full titles are often lengthy, they will be abbreviated in the list, but first their full names and abbreviations are listed here with thanks and appreciation.

American: American Geographical Society, New York

Australia: National Library of Australia, Canberra

Bishop: The Bernice P. Bishop Museum, Honolulu

British: The British Museum, London

Grimble: Sir A. Grimble and the Royal Navy Intelligence Handbook, Vol. 1

Harvard: The Peabody Museum Library, Harvard University, Cambridge

MacLean: Robert MacLean (artist), Putney, Vermont

Marine: Musee de la Marine, Paris

Maritime: The National Maritime Museum, Greenwich

Mitchell: The Mitchell Library, Sydney

Neuchatel: Musee d'Ethnographie, Neuchatel

NYPL: The New York Public Library

Oglesby: Albert Oglesby (photographer), Putney, Vermont

Paris: Admiral F. E. Paris, from his book, see Bibliography

Pitt-Rivers: The Pitt-Rivers Museum, Oxford

Polynesia: The Polynesian Society, Wellington

Salem: The Peabody Museum Library, Salem

Shore: Edward Shore (photographer), Putney, Vermont

Stockholm: Ethnografiska Museet, Stockholm

Tattersall: Tattersall's Studio, Apia

T = top, M = middle, B = bottom

page	Frontis	Parkinson, *British*	28-29	*MacLean*
	19	Sauer, *American*, 1952	31	Emory and Sinoto, *Bishop*
	21	Webber, *Mitchell*	34	Handy, *Bishop*
	22	Webber, *Maritime*	35-37	Stimson, *Salem*

38		Young, *Polynesia*	108		D'Urville, *Oglesby*
48		*MacLean*	110	T	Webber, *Mitchell*
49		*MacLean*	110	B	Buck, *Bishop*
51		*Shore*	111		Wilkes (2 pictures)
58-59		D. Lewis, *MacLean*	112	T	Beechey, *Oglesby*
64		Tupaia, *British*	112	B	Hornell, *Tattersall*
68	T	Hornell, *Bishop*	113	T	Webber, *Bishop*
68	B	*Paris*	113	B	Webber, *NYPL*
69	T	Choris, *Bishop*	114-115		Webber, *Bishop*
69	B	Ellis, *Oglesby*	116		Webber, *Maritime*
70		Ellis, *Oglesby*	118		Handy (3 pictures), *Bishop*
71	T	Hawkesworth, *Oglesby*	120		Wallis (3 pictures), *British*
71	B	Cook, *NYPL*	121		Hornell, *Bishop*
72		Lescallier, *NYPL*	122	T	*Neuchatel*
74		Schouten (2 pictures), *NYPL*	122	B	*Salem*
75		Tasman, *Harvard*	123	T	*Pitt-Rivers*
76	T	Tasman, *Harvard*	123	B	*Pitt-Rivers*
76	B	Anonymous, after Tasman, *NYPL*	124	T	*Bishop*
			124	B	*Marine*
77	T	Hodges, *Mitchell*	125	T	*Salem*
77	B	Hodges, *British*	125	B	*Pitt-Rivers*
78	T	Webber, *British*	127		Unsigned, first voyage, *British*
78	B	Labillardiere, *Oglesby*	129		Bougainville, *NYPL*
79		D'Urville, *Oglesby*	130	T	Webber, *Maritime*
80	T	D'Urville, *Mitchell*	130	B	Webber, *Australia*, from the original in the Rex Nan Kivell collection
80	B	D'Urville, *Oglesby*			
84-88		Parkinson (6 pictures), *British*			
89	T	Spöring, *British*	131		Hodges, *Mitchell*
89	T&B	Tyerman, *Oglesby*	132	T	Hodges, *British*
90		Hodges, *Maritime*	132	B	Hodges, *NYPL*
91		Hodges, *British*	133	T	Hodges, *Mitchell*
92	B	Hodges, *British*	133	M	D'Urville, *Mitchell*
92	M	Roberts, *Mitchell*	133	B	Langsdorff, *Oglesby*
92	T	Roberts, *Mitchell*	134	T	Webber, *Maritime*
93	T	Webber, *British*	134	B	D'Urville, *Mitchell*
93	B	Webber, *British*	135		D'Urville, *Oglesby*
94-95		Webber, *British*	136		Webber, *British*
96	T	Webber, *Maritime*	137		*Bishop*
96	B	Webber, *British*	138		*Grimble*
97	T	Cleveley, *Oglesby*	139		Webber, *Maritime*
97	M	Cleveley, *Oglesby*	140	T	Cook, *Mitchell*
97	B	*Duff*, *Oglesby*	140	M	Cook, *Mitchell*
98	T	Bligh, *Mitchell*	140	B	Cook, *NYPL*
98	M	Tobin, *Mitchell*	141		Cook, *NYPL*
98	B	Tobin, *Mitchell*	142-152		*Paris* (8 plans)
102		Tasman, *Harvard*	153		Langsdorff
103		Hawkesworth, *Oglesby*	155		*Stockholm*
104	T	Hodges, *Mitchell*	164		*MacLean* after Walton and Savage, *Using The Sky*
104	B	Hodges, *Mitchell*			
105	T	Hodges, *British*	165		*MacLean*
105	B	Hodges, *Maritime*	166		Heyen, *Polynesia*
106		*Bishop*	169-173		Henry, *Bishop*
107		Henry (chant), *Bishop*	174		*MacLean*

Bibliography

This is an informal, personal, and perhaps at times, even prejudiced bibliography of books, sources, and individuals that I have found particularly helpful in compiling this book. In most cases, especially in those of well known writers, "various works" are listed. Professor C. R. H. Taylor's A PACIFIC BIBLIOGRAPHY will list them all for anyone wishing to look farther. Moreover he has organized them so ingeniously in subject matter, geographical groups, etc. that with a little browsing one can find anything he wants. His work is an indispensable tool for any serious study of Oceania and it would be presumptuous (and impossible) to compete with it.

Akerblom, Kjell. *Astronomy and Navigation in Polynesia and Micronesia*. Etnografiska Museet, Stockholm, 1968. This thorough and painstaking monograph has been commented on sufficiently in the text.

Arago, J. E. V. Various works. Arago was one of the early artists who travelled about the world, notably with Freycinet. His canoes were more works of art than of accuracy.

Bancroft, H. H. was a well known and well respected American historian. His work dealt principally with the American Indian cultures of the Pacific coast.

Banks, Sir Joseph. *Journals 1768 - 1771* was of course the patron and at times the bane of Cook on his first voyage. His was a rich personality and he presided over the flowering of science in the England of his day. A most excellently annotated edition of his *Journal* has been recently produced by J. C. Beaglehole.

Barrau, J. Various works. Probably the first authority today on the agricultural aspects of Polynesia.

Beaglehole, Earnest and Pearl. *Ethnology of Pukapuka* Bishop Museum Bulletin no. 150, 1938. One of the very best first-hand reports on sailing by stars.

Beaglehole, J. C. His meticulous and imaginative researches on all aspects of Cook's voyages, especially on unpublished illustrative materials, have been invaluable in producing this specialized work on canoes.

Bechtol, C. *Sailing Characteristics of Oceanic Canoes* in "Polynesian Navigation," Jack Golson, editor. Polynesian Society, 1963. An interesting article on the results of careful experiments with 30 inch models of double canoes.

Beechey, F. W. *Voyage . . . in the Blossom*, 1825-28. The best source of information on Polynesian (Mangareva) rafts.

Best, Elsdon. Various, nay multitudinous, works, mostly Maori, mostly folklore, but wide ranging. Best was one of the early anthropologists to specialize in Polynesia.

Bisschop, E. de, *Tahiti Nui*, London 1959. A highly emotional account of his building and sailing a somewhat unlikely raft.

Bligh, William. *Voyage . . . in the 'Bounty'*, 1792. Everyone knows about the mutiny, but few realize that he drew the picture of the double canoe on page 98.

Boenechea, D. *Voyage* 1772 - 73. The first Spaniard to visit Tahiti. See also Varela.

Bougainville, L. A. *Voyage . . . in the frigate "La Boudeuse"* 1766 - 1769. The second European to visit Tahiti and the first to record a Society Island canoe, page 129.

Bryan, E. H. Various articles. One of our foremost authorities on Polynesian stars and star lore.

Buck, Sir Peter H. (Te Rangi Hiroa). Many works. Next to Hornell, Dr. Buck has been the most valuable authority for this book. His mother was a Maori so Polynesian was his natural tongue. He was accepted everywhere and could collect information available to no other anthropologist. As a staff member and later director of the Bishop Museum for many years he was sent on many scientific expeditions throughout Polynesia. His particular interest was material culture and his large exhaustive and carefully detailed books are a basic library in themselves.

Carlquist, Sherwin. *Island Life*, Natural History Press, New York, 1965. An excellent book on the special characteristics of life on isolated islands. Nothing about man, but it has meaning for him.

Choris, Louis. *Voyage, etc.* 1822. The artist on Kotzebue's voyage.

Churchill, William. *Weather Words of Polynesia*, American Anthropology Association Memoir vol 2. No 1, 1907.

Cleveley. James Cleveley was Cook's ship's carpenter on his third voyage. He had a brother John in London who was an artist and evidently James collected some raw material in the south seas for brother John to work up. The results as noted on page 97 were decidedly mixed from a nautical point of view, but they resulted in three pleasant island scenes and a dramatic depiction of the death of Cook.

Cook, James. *Journals*. These are too widely known to need comment here, only a reminder that the recent edition annotated by J. C. Beaglehole is a godsend to any modern scholar, especially for its exhaustive index. *Vol I first voyage, 1955, Vol II second voyage, 1961, Vols III and IV third voyage, 1967.*

Danielsson, Bengt. Various works. First hand information from a long-time resident.

Davies, John and D. Darling. *A Tahitian and English Dictionary, 1851*. The only good early record of the Tahitian language. Many old terms no longer in use revealing the character and quality of the Polynesian mind. It is much earlier than the publication date indicates for it was delayed some 25 years getting into print.

Dening, G. M. *The Geographical Knowledge of the Polynesians and the Nature of Inter-Island Contact* in "Polynesian Navigation," J. Golson, editor. An excellent summary on the side of deliberate voyaging.

Dodge, Ernest. Various works. The latest, *"Beyond the Capes,"* 1971 fills many gaps in reviewing the lesser known voyages.

Duff, Roger. *The Moa Hunter Period of Maori Culture* 1956 and various other works. Director of the Canterbury Museum, Dr. Duff is one of the outstanding anthropologists of New Zealand and the leading authority on adzes.

Duff, (ship). The first missionary voyage to the south seas 1796 - 98 commanded by Captain James Wilson is one of the best early records.

D'Urville, Dumont. *Two voyages, 1826 - 29 and 1837 - 40*. From a scientific point of view these big handsome publications are by far the best work of the French explorers. See Index.

Edge-Partington, J. *Album in 3 vols, 1890*. A comprehensive set of drawings of all sorts of artifacts.

Elbert, S. H. Various works, mostly on folklore and linguistics.

Ellis, William. *Polynesian Researches*, 4 vols. 1831. A mine of information after 8 years residence, somewhat biased by missionary zeal, but good on material culture and sailing.

Emory, Kenneth P. A huge body of work by the foremost living anthropologist and archaeologist of Polynesia. For a bibliography of over 100 items see the late volume by his colleagues celebrating his 70th birthday, "Polynesian Culture History" 1967. I have learned more from Emory's work than from that of any other man especially in the navigational aspects of this book, but he has also done much pioneering on canoes.

Finney, Ben. Various works. One of the younger anthropologists who is testing theories in the field with the latest scientific equipment.

Firth, R. A large body of work, best known for his field work in Tikopia, but ranging widely on all aspects of Polynesian life.

Force, R. W. Director of the Bishop Museum in Honolulu. He presides over the many projects and exhibits in that foremost center of Pacific research.

Fornander, A. *An Account of the Polynesian Race, Its Origin and Migrations, 3 vols. 1878 - 85*. A huge compilation of important material deriving mostly from Hawaii.

Frankel, J. P. Various articles on Polynesian navigation notably in "Navigation" Vol 9, no. 1, 1962. Chief exponent of the star compass theory.

Garanger, J. Various articles notably on pottery.

Gatty, Harold. *The Raft Book*, 1943. *Nature is Your Guide*, 1958. See comments in text.

Gill, W. W. Various works. A missionary who cared about and recorded customs, legends, etc. good on winds and stars.

Golson, Jack. *Polynesian Navigation* (editor) 1963 "A Symposium on Andrew Sharp's Theory of Accidental Voyaging" . . . and a very lively one.

Goodenough, W. *Native Astronomy in the Central Carolines*, University of Penna. Museum Monograph 1953 and various other works. Another advocate of the star compass.

Green, Roger. Various works by one of the best contemporary archaeologists.

Grey, Sir George. *Polynesian Mythology* 1855. One of the earliest and best collections of Maori lore by a former Governor of New Zealand 1846 - 54 and 1861 - 67.

Grimble, Sir A. *Canoes of the Gilbert Islands* 1924 and many other works; perhaps the foremost authority on the Gilberts.

Hamilton, A. *The Art Workmanship of the Maori Race*, 1896. The best of its kind and date.

Handy, E. S. C. *The Native Culture in the Marquesas* 1923 and many other works. One of the best ethnologists of his day.

Hawkesworth, J. *Account of the Voyages . . . of Byron, Wallis, Carteret and Cook*, 1773. An eminent and popular literary figure, the chief proponent of the great "southern continent" theory.

Henry, Teuira. *Ancient Tahiti*, 1928. See page 169.

Heyen, G. H. *Primitive Navigation in the Pacific - I* in "Polynesian Navigation," Golson, J. editor. See especially his comment on the *Pedersen* voyage pages 166 - 167.

Heyerdahl, T. *Kon Tiki, Aku Aku* etc. The foremost advocate of drift migration and of settlement from America.

Hilder, B. *Primitive Navigation in the Pacific - II* in "Polynesian Navigation," J. Golson, editor. He is much excited about navigational stones.

Hodges, William. The artist on Cook's second voyage, 1772 - 1775. See Index.

Hornell, James. *Canoes of Oceania*, 1936. Vol I Canoes of Polynesia, Fiji, and Micronesia. The standard and by far the most exhaustive work on the subject. This book has been drawn on more heavily than any other reference work. See Index.

Jourdain, P. J. The table of the principal voyages of discovery in the Appendix is an expanded version of Commandant Jourdain's table in the "Bulletin de la Societe des Etudes Oceanienne" Vol XIV, no 10, no. 171 Juin 1970.

Kamakau, S. M. *Hawaiian Astronomy*, 1891.

Kotzebue, Otto von. *A New Voyage . . .*, 1823 - 6. One of Krusenstern's officers who made a successful Russian circumnavigation.

Kramer, A. *Die Samoa - Inseln* 2 vols. 1902 and many other works, all in German. Thorough and reliable.

Krusenstern, A. J. *Voyage* 1803 - 06, 2 vol. The first Russian circumnavigator and one of the most productive expeditions from a scientific point of view.

Labillardiere, J. J. *Voyage in Search of La Perouse* 2 vols 1791 - 94.

Langsdorff, G. H. *Voyages* etc. 2 vols, 1803 - 7. A member of Krusenstern's company. See Index.

La Perouse, J. F. G. de, *Voyage in 1785 - 8*, 3 vols. The great French navigator who was lost with all hands.

Le Maire, I. The patron of Schouten's voyage in 1615. His son Jacob sailed as supercargo.

Lescallier, M. *Traité du Gréement*, 1791. A textbook on rigging with some interesting though second-hand illustrations of Polynesian canoes.

Lewis, David. *An Experiment in Polynesian Navigation*, Journal of Institute of Navigation vol 19 No. 2, April 1966. Lewis's account of his voyage in the double hulled *Rehu - Moana* from Tahiti to New Zealand navigating without instruments. A pioneering work that has caused much controversy and whose theories are now being further tested and refined in Micronesian waters.

Lewthwaite, Gordon. *Geographical Knowledge of the Pacific Peoples* in "The Pacific Basin," H. R. Friis (ed) 1967. One of the very best reviews of the subject.

Linton, R. *Material Culture of the Marquesas*, 1923 and other works. With Emory and Handy, Linton was one of the best anthropologists of his time.

Lisianski, U. *Voyage . . . etc* 1803 - 06. A member of Krusenstern's expedition, the first Russian circumnavigation.

Makemson, Maud. *The Morning Star Rises* 1941 "An account of Polynesian Astronomy." Somewhat romanticized, but a most interesting book.

Mariner, W. *An Account of the Natives of the Tonga Islands*, etc. 1817. The best book on early Tonga. Mariner stayed there four years c. 1806 - 10. One of the early "as told to's," (John Martin).

Mendana, A. d., *Narrative of Voyage . . . 1595 - 6 . . . by P. F. de Quiros*. The earliest of the Spanish explorers to touch Polynesia.

Métraux, A. *Ethnology of Easter Island,* 1940. Probably the best work on this island.

Moerenhout, J. A. *Voyages etc* 2 vols. 1837. Particularly good on the outlying islands of central Polynesia.

Monberg, T. with Elbert S. *From the Two Canoes* 1965, Copenhagen. A brilliant young anthropologist who has worked mostly in the Polynesian outliers in Melanesia.

Mulloy, W. Various articles about Easter Island. Responsible for most of the present restoration work. Originally a member of the Heyerdahl expedition.

Natua, Aurora. Custodian of the Papeete Museum.

Oliver, Douglas. *The Pacific Islands* 1951. A review of their history by a distinguished scholar. And other works.

O'Reilly, Patrick. Numerous works by this outstanding priest, bibliographer, and savant.

Orsmund, J. M. of the London Missionary Society resident in various islands of Polynesia from 1817 to 1856, was the collector of the materials which enabled Teuira Henry to compile *Ancient Tahiti* 1928.

Paris, F. E. *Essai sur la construction navale des peuples extra-européens etc.* 2 vols 1843. Most of the plans, pages 142 - 152 were taken from Admiral Paris's splendid big volume.

Parkinson, Sydney. *Journal . . . 1773.* He was the artist on Cook's first voyage. See Index.

Parsonson, G. S. *The Settlement of Oceania* in "Polynesian Navigation," Golson, J. editor. 1963. An excellent review of the subject. One of the best.

Petit - Thouars, A. du, *Voyage 1836 - 39,* 4 vols and atlas. This gentleman took possession of the Marquesas and Society and other central Island groups for France.

Porter, D. *Voyage 1812 - 1814.* One of the earliest Americans to visit the Marquesas.

Quiros, P. F. de, *Voyages 1595 - 1606.* Mendana's pilot and later successor.

Radiguet, M. *Les Derniers Sauvages,* 1860. The author spent 17 years in the Marquesas.

Reche, E. *Die Dreisternnavigation der Polynesier,* 1927. A very complicated theory based on the revolving of three-star triangles. It seems to me much too trigonometrical for a Polynesian.

Roberts, Henry. A seaman on Cook's second voyage who joined at the age of 15 and showed a fine talent for drawing and chart work. See page 92.

Robertson, George. *The Discovery of Tahiti etc. 1766 - 68.* The master of Wallis's *Dolphin,* quoted frequently in the text.

Roggeveen, J. *Voyage 1721 - 22.* The discoverer of Easter Island and the first to record their canoes, simple outrigger types that were too small to go far to sea.

Rollin, L. *Ancienne Civilization Marquisiene,* 1953. A doctor's reminiscenses refreshingly non religious.

Routledge, Mrs. C. S. *The Mystery of Easter Island,* 1917. A standard book principally on the *ahu* and great stone figures.

Saint-Hilaire, Marcq. An early 20th Century navigator who developed the standard method adopted by the US Hydrographic office (Bowditch) and used for many years between the two world wars.

Sauer, Carl O. *Agricultural Origins and Dispersals*, 1952 and many other works. Chairman of the Dept. of Geography University of California, Berkeley. See page 19.

Schouten, W. Captain & navigator of the *Eendracht*, probably the first European vessel to visit a Tongan island in 1614.

Sebastian, Father Englert. *Island At The Center of the World*, 1970. Recollections and studies of a priest who lived 34 years on the Island.

Shapiro, Harry. Numerous works especially in the field of physical anthropology.

Sharp, Andrew. *Ancient Voyagers in the Pacific*, 1956, later revised and expanded following the publication of "Polynesian Navigation," Golson, J. editor. Professor Sharp is an excellent historian, viz his "The Discovery of the Pacific Islands," 1960 and "The Voyages of Abel Jansoon Tasman," 1968. I just wish he would forget his accidental obsession.

Sinoto, Yosi. *Prehistoric Culture in Oceania*, 1968 and various other works. Now chief of the Dept. of Anthropology at the Bishop Museum, Sinoto is one of the best and most vigorous archaeologists at work in Polynesia.

Skinner, H. D. Numerous writings on all aspects of Polynesian culture. Until his retirement a few years ago, Dr. Skinner was generally considered the dean of all anthropologists specializing in Polynesia.

Smith, Isaac. Admiral Smith was a member of Cook's company and a noted collector of early documents pertaining to Oceania. The early plans for Cook's war canoe see page 140 are in his collection at the Mitchell Library in Sydney.

Smith, S. Percy. Numerous works mostly on the Maori. Like Elsdon Best, Percy Smith was one of the early and prolific collectors.

Spoehr, A. Various articles by the former Director of the Bishop Museum and a leading American anthropologist.

Spöring, H. D. The Swedish assistant naturalist on Cook's first voyage, was, says Dr. Beaglehole, a draughtsman of great ability. See page 89.

Tasman, A. J. *Journal 1642 - 43.* A Dutchman, one of the earliest and best known of the Pacific explorers. See pages 75 - 76 and 102.

Taylor, E. G. R. *The Haven-Finding Art, a History of Navigation from Odysseus to Captain Cook*, 1956. Nothing about Polynesia, but an excellent review of navigation in the western world.

Titcomb, M. *Voyage of the Flying Bird*, 1963 and other works. A reconstruction of the settlement of Hawaii.

Tobin, George. *Journal 1791 - 93.* Bligh's 3rd lieutenant on his second voyage was an industrious and fairly accomplished artist. See page 98.

Tumarkin, D. D. and V. Voitov. *Navigational Conditions of Sea Routes to Polynesia*, Asian and Pacific Archeology Series No. 1, 1967, Golheim, W. G. editor. A Russian study of the "South Equatorial Countercurrent."

Tyerman, D. and G. Bennet, *Journal*, 1821 - 29.

Tylor, Sir Edward B. *Primitive Culture*, 1871. Paul Radin says Tylor created modern anthropology "practically from its foundations."

Vancouver, George. *Voyage 1790 - 95* 3 vols. An officer of Cook's and later commander of his own expedition. A basic book on early Polynesia.

Van Dorn, W. G. *Oceanography and Seamanship for Mariners*, in press.

Varela, J. de A. y, *Journal 1774 - 5.* See Corney, B. G. *The Quest and Occupation of Tahiti* 1915. The Hakluyt Society. Accompanied Boenechea on his second voyage.

184

Vayda, A. P. (editor) *Peoples and Cultures of the Pacific*, 1968. An up-to-date symposium.

Villiers, Alan. *Captain James Cook*, 1967. The quote on page 176 is from his National Geographic book.

von den Steinen, *Die Marquesaner und irhe Kunst* 3 vols, 1925 - 8. A thorough basic study of the Marquesas. His volume on "Tatauiering" is the best of any.

Wallace, A. R. *The Polynesians and their Migrations*, 1900 and other works. One of the great pioneers.

Wallis, S. *Journal 1766 - 8* unpublished in the Mitchell library, but there is an account of the voyage of the *Dolphin* in Hawkesworth.

Webber, James. *Views in the South Seas* and most of the illustrations for Cook's 3rd voyage. See Index for plates in this book.

White, John. *The Ancient History of the Maori* 6 vols, 1889. A monumental work by the diligent secretary of Sir George Grey.

Whitney, H. P. *An Analysis of the Design of the Major Seagoing Craft of Oceania*, 1955. An unpublished thesis for a master's degree at the University of Pennsylvania. Some original and imaginative thinking.

Wilkes, C. *Narrative of U.S. Exploring Expedition 1833 - 42, 5 vols and atlas*. A widely known work but not much on navigation or canoes.

Williams, John. *Narrative of Missionary Enterprizes etc.*, 1837. He travelled around a lot and was a keen observer.

Wilson, James. *Missionary Voyages 1796 - 8 in the Ship "Duff."* Wilson's own section of this book is particularly useful. He was a professional sea captain hired to sail the missionaries to their islands.

PRINCIPAL VOYAGES OF DISCOVERY AND EXPLORATION IN POLYNESIA

	English	American	Spanish	French	Dutch	Russian
16th Century						
1521			Magellan			
1595			Mendana			
17th Century						
1605			Quiros			
1616					Le Maire & Schouten	
1642					Tasman	
18th Century						
1722						Roggeveen
1765	Byron					
1767	Wallis Carteret					
1768				Bougainville		
1769	Cook 1st Voyage					
1772			Boenechea			
1773-1774	Cook 2nd Voyage					
1774-1775			Boenechea plus Gayangos Varela			
1777	Cook 3rd Voyage					
1785				La Perouse		
1788-1789	Bligh 1st Voyage					
1791	Edwards Vancouver	Ingraham		Marchand		
1792		Roberts	Malaspina	D'Entre-casteaux		
1793	Bligh 2nd Voyage					
1797	Wilson					
19th Century						
1804						Krusenstern
1812-1814		Porter				
1816						Kotzebue 1st Voyage
1817				Freycinet		
1820						Bellingshausen
1823				Duperrey		
1824						Kotzebue 2nd Voyage
1825-1826	Beechey					
1835	Fitz-Roy					
1836	Russel					
1838				Dumont d'Urville Dupetit Thouars		
1838-1842		Wilkes				

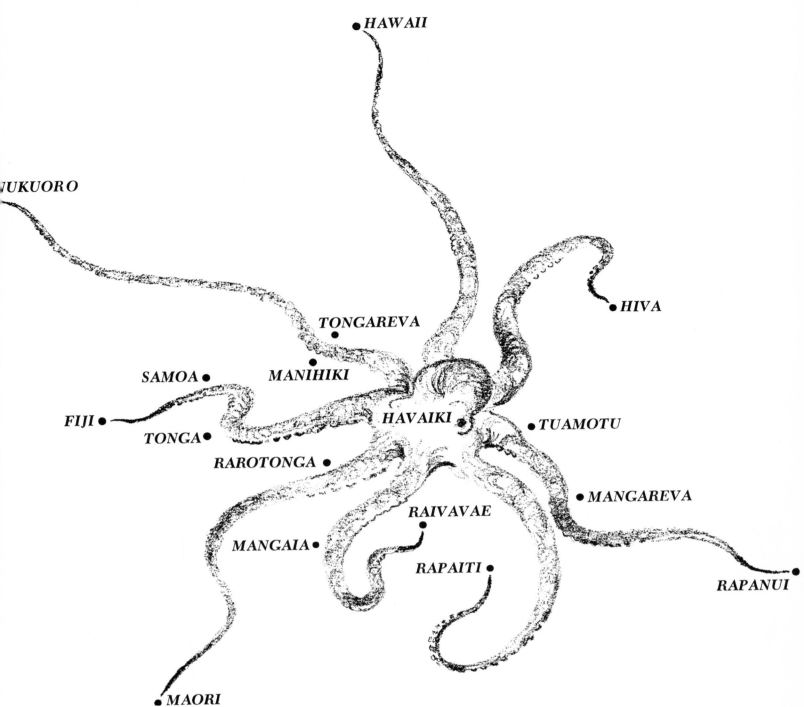

HAWAII

NUKUORO

HIVA

TONGAREVA

SAMOA

MANIHIKI

FIJI

HAVAIKI

TUAMOTU

TONGA

RAROTONGA

MANGAREVA

RAIVAVAE

RAPANUI

MANGAIA

RAPAITI

MAORI

From the core and later the central island groups of Polynesia; Samoa, Tonga, Fiji, then Tahiti, Rarotonga; colonists went forth like the tentacles of an octopus to settle the distant peripheral groups; the Hivas, Rapanui, Hawaii, and Maoriland. It is a recognized axiom of human migration that those who leave the homeland take with them the basic ancestral customs and not only hang on to them stubbornly but tend to develop them even to a rococo stage or to an elaboration that becomes degenerate. While the original core culture tends to let old forms disappear, the outlying and disconnected nuclei of the parent culture develop their own fanciful variants on the original theme.

The parent culture on the "map" is designated Havaiki, the Polynesian's name for his ancestral home. It comprised what we call the Society Island group with its best known island, Tahiti, and its "Holy Land," Raiatea.

Index

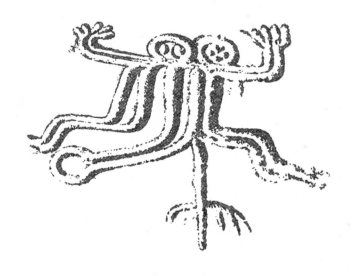